☙ INTERVENTIONISM

The Liberty Fund Library of the Works of
Ludwig von Mises

Theory and History: An Interpretation of Social
and Economic Evolution
Liberalism: The Classical Tradition
Human Action: A Treatise on Economics
The Ultimate Foundation of Economic Science: An Essay
on Method
Nation, State, and Economy: Contributions to the Politics
and History of Our Time
The Anti-capitalistic Mentality
Economic Freedom and Interventionism: An Anthology
of Articles and Essays
Bureaucracy
Planning for Freedom: Let the Market System Work
A Collection of Essays and Addresses
Economic Policy: Thoughts for Today and Tomorrow
Interventionism: An Economic Analysis
Omnipotent Government: The Rise of the Total State
and Total War
On the Manipulation of Money and Credit: Three
Treatises on Trade-Cycle Theory

LUDWIG VON MISES

Interventionism

An Economic Analysis

 LUDWIG VON MISES

Edited and with a Foreword by Bettina Bien Greaves

LIBERTY FUND   *Indianapolis*

This book is published by Liberty Fund, Inc., a foundation established to encourage study of the ideal of a society of free and responsible individuals.

𒂼𒄄

The cuneiform inscription that serves as our logo and as the design motif for our endpapers is the earliest-known written appearance of the word "freedom" (*amagi*), or "liberty." It is taken from a clay document written about 2300 B.C. in the Sumerian city-state of Lagash.

Interventionism was written by Ludwig von Mises in 1940 and is here translated from the original German by Thomas Francis McManus and Heinrich Bund.

Editorial additions and index © 1998, 2011 by Liberty Fund, Inc.

Interventionism was originally published in 1998 by Foundation for Economic Education, Inc.

Front cover photograph of Ludwig von Mises used by permission of the Ludwig von Mises Institute, Auburn, Alabama
Frontispiece courtesy of Bettina Bien Greaves
All rights reserved

Printed in the United States of America

C 10 9 8 7 6 5 4 3 2 1
P 10 9 8 7 6 5 4 3 2 1

Library of Congress Cataloging-in-Publication Data

Von Mises, Ludwig, 1881–1973.
  Interventionism: an economic analysis / Ludwig von Mises; edited and with a foreword by Bettina Bien Greaves.
    p. cm.
  "Originally published in 1998 by Foundation for Economic Education, Inc."
  Includes bibliographical references and index.
  ISBN 978-0-86597-738-9 (hardcover: alk. paper)—
  ISBN 978-0-86597-739-6 (pbk.: alk. paper)
  1. Economic policy. 2. Central planning. I. Greaves, Bettina Bien. II. Title.
  HD87.5 .V66 2011
  330.15′7—dc22

                                        2008029309

Liberty Fund, Inc.
8335 Allison Pointe Trail, Suite 300
Indianapolis, Indiana 46250–1684

CONTENTS

Ludwig von Mises lived a long life—from 1881 to 1973. He was born within the borders of the huge European empire of Austria-Hungary and was for many years the leading spokesman of what became known as the Austrian School of Economics. This theoretical school differs from other schools of economics because it does not deal with aggregates, large numbers, or historical data. It uses a *micro* rather than a *macro* approach to economics. It traces all economic phenomena back to the actions of individuals—to their subjective values and to the value each market participant places on the marginal utility of a particular good or service. The Austrians view the world economy as a giant auction in which everyone is always bidding for the various goods and services he or she wants by offering something he or she has. By starting from the viewpoint of the individual actor and by reasoning logically step by step, Mises and his fellow Austrian economists were able to explain the development of prices, wages, money, production, trade, and so on.

Mises was prolific. He wrote many books and articles. He traveled and lectured widely throughout Europe and gained an international reputation as a strong advocate of capitalism and an ardent critic of interventionism. However, Mises's teachings were drowned out for many years by the overwhelming popularity of John Maynard Keynes, Keynes's macroeconomic doctrines, and his proposals for government intervention and politically expedient spending programs.

Mises left Vienna for Switzerland before the Germans, under Hitler, occupied Austria. He taught in Geneva at the Institute for International Studies until 1940, when he migrated to the United States. His reputation had been well established in Europe. But when he arrived in this country at age 59, he was a stranger in a strange land, obliged to start almost all over again. He soon obtained an appointment at the National Bureau of Economic Research, which gave him the opportunity to write the manuscript for this book.

Anyone who is familiar with Mises's other writings will not find anything particularly surprising in this book. Mises frequently criticized the various aspects of government intervention and he often described how government intervention interferes with the attempts of individuals to accomplish their various goals. However, in none of his other writings does he explain government intervention and its consequences more clearly and simply than he does here.

Mises wrote *Interventionism: An Economic Analysis** in his native German tongue. After it had been translated by Drs. Thomas McManus and Heinrich Bund, he considered it "ready for publication." However, apparently nothing was done about the manuscript and it disappeared from view. When this project came to nought, Mises, of necessity, turned his efforts toward other writing and lecturing. In 1944, his *Bureaucracy* and *Omnipotent Government* were published. In 1945, he received an appointment as visiting professor at New York University Graduate School of Business Administration and began teaching again. Then in 1946, he joined the staff of the Foundation for Economic Education as a part-time adviser. Many other books followed, including especially his magnum opus, *Human Action*, in 1949.

This book, *Interventionism*, was written in 1940, before the United States was officially involved in World War II. Here Mises offers a rare insight into the war economies of Hitler's Germany and Mussolini's Italy. He also criticizes the pre–World War II Allied governments for having favored socialism and interventionism over capitalist methods of production. As a matter of fact, he blames the Allies' lack of military preparedness on their having fallen prey to anti-capitalist propaganda and for having spent more effort trying to prevent war profiteering than on creating an economic climate conducive to the production of armaments. "When the capitalist nations in time of war give up the industrial superiority which their economic system provides them, their power to resist and their chances to win are considerably reduced. . . . The defeat of France and the destruction of English cities

---

* In spite of the similar title, Mises's *Critique of Interventionism* (1929; English translation, 1977) is a very different book from this one. That book is an anthology of articles criticizing the doctrines and proposals of specific interventionists of the 1920s; this book is a clear and simple exposition of the theory of government intervention.

was the first price paid for the interventionist suppression of war profits" (pp. 76, 77).

Throughout his career, Mises pointed out that individuals face risk and uncertainty in their struggle to survive. They encounter many obstacles—both natural and man-made. Natural catastrophes such as earthquakes, floods, tornadoes, hurricanes, landslides, avalanches, and fires may disrupt their plans. Man-made catastrophes such as wars, theft, fraud, and government interventions may also disrupt their plans. With respect to the obstacles nature places in their paths, men have no alternative but to cope as best they can. With respect to man-made obstacles, however, the situation is different; men are not completely helpless; they have the capability of avoiding and/or removing them.

In explaining how the market functions, Mises criticized man-made government interventions—controls, regulations, restrictions, special privileges, and subsidies for some at the expense of others. He always pointed out, as he does in this book, that although enacted with the best of intentions, such government interventions lead to conditions that even their advocates consider worse than those they were trying to alleviate. However, he also explained that such obstacles, being man-made, were avoidable and removable—once people came to realize that government should not interfere with peaceful interpersonal relationships.

Mises also pointed out that government's role should be limited. Government should protect equally the lives and property of all persons under its jurisdiction. It should adjudicate disputes among individuals so as to assure, insofar as possible, equal justice to all. Otherwise, it should leave people free to work out their own destinies. We are fortunate indeed that this manuscript, which explains in such clear terms these basic principles, has resurfaced from among the papers left at Mises's death and is now being made available.

Bettina Bien Greaves
October 1997

It is the purpose of this essay to analyze the problems of government interference in business from the economic standpoint. The political and social consequences of the policy of interventionism[1] can only be understood and judged on the basis of an understanding of its economic implications and effects.

Ever since the European governments in the last decades of the nineteenth century embarked on this policy, which today frequently is called "progressive" but which actually represents a return to the mercantilist policy of the seventeenth and early eighteenth centuries, economists have persistently pointed out the inconsistency and futility of these measures and have predicted their political and social consequences. Governments, political parties, and public opinion have just as persistently ignored their warnings. They ridiculed the alleged doctrinarism of "orthodox" economics and boasted of their "victories" over economic theory. But these were Pyrrhic victories.

The inevitable sequence of events which followed upon the application of interventionist measures fully proved the correctness of the economists' predictions. The predicted political effects, social unrest, dictatorship, and war, also did not fail to appear.

This essay is not intended to discuss specifically the American New Deal. It deals with interventionism in general, and its conclusions are valid for all instances of interventionism irrespective of the country concerned. There was a considerable amount of interventionism in America long before 1933. The New Deal is merely the present-day, specifically American brand of a policy which began everywhere—including

---

1. Throughout this essay, the term interventionism is used in the sense ascribed to it by many generations of economists. It covers the domestic policy of governmental interference with business. It is not to be confused with the political term "interventionism" referring to international policy, as contrasted with "isolationism" in the current American controversy about the War.

America—several decades ago. To the economist there is nothing new in the New Deal. It differs from the policy of Kaiser Wilhelm II and from the policy of the Weimar Republic only to the extent necessitated by the particular conditions of present-day America. And it places the American people today in the same dilemma in which the German people found themselves ten years ago.

This essay is economic in character and, therefore, is not concerned with the legal and constitutional aspects of the problem. Laws and constitutions as such are of secondary importance only. They are to serve the people, not to rule the people. They are to be formulated and interpreted in such a way as to make possible an economic development beneficial to the welfare of all groups of the nation. If they fail to reach this aim, the laws and their interpretation ought to be changed.

There is certainly no lack of literature on this subject; almost every day new contributions appear. But almost all of these studies are concerned exclusively with particular groups of measures and their short-run effects. This method of analysis is woefully inadequate. It merely shows the immediate consequences of individual interventions without considering their indirect and long-run effects. It takes into account only the alleged benefits and disregards the costs and detriments.

In this way, of course, a comprehensive appraisal of the social and economic consequences of interventionism can never be reached. That certain individuals or small groups of individuals may sometimes be temporarily privileged or benefited by certain interventionist measures cannot be denied. The question is, however, what further effects are caused, particularly if the attempt is made to accord in the same way privileges to large sections of the population or even to the whole nation. It is therefore essential to study the totality of interventionist policy, not only its short-run but also its long-run effects.

It would be a thorough misinterpretation of my statements to consider them as a criticism of the statesmen and politicians in power. My criticism is not aimed at men, but at a doctrine. No matter what the constitution of the country, governments always have to pursue that policy which is deemed right and beneficial by popular opinion. Were they to attempt to stand up against the prevailing doctrines they would very soon lose their positions to men willing to conform to the demands of the man in the street. Dictators too can only seize and maintain power if they are backed by the approval of the masses. The totalitarianism of our times is the product of the wide acceptance of totalitarian ideology; it can only be overcome by a different philosophy.

If we are to understand economic problems, we have to keep ourselves free of all prejudices and preconceived opinions. If we are convinced beforehand that the measures which are being recommended to benefit certain groups or classes, for instance laborers or farmers, actually do benefit and do not injure those groups, and if we are determined not to abandon our prejudices, we shall never learn anything. It is the very task of economic analysis to ascertain whether the policies recommended by the various parties and pressure groups actually lead to the results which their advocates desire.

The problem is not whether the capitalist system (i.e., the market economy) is good or bad. The real question is whether it would be in the interest of the masses of the people to replace the market economy with another system. When someone points out some unfavorable conditions which the market economy has not been able to eliminate he has by no means proved the practicability and desirability of either interventionism or socialism.

This certainly is still the least objectionable argumentation. As a rule, capitalism is blamed for the undesired effects of a policy directed at its elimination. The man who sips his morning coffee does not say, "Capitalism has brought this beverage to my breakfast table." But when he reads in the papers that the government of Brazil has ordered part of the coffee crop destroyed, he does not say, "That is government for you"; he exclaims, "That is capitalism for you."

An analysis of the problems with which this book is concerned must be conducted strictly according to the rules of logic and has to avoid everything that might disturb the objective judgment by appeal to the emotions. Consequently I have refrained from making this essay more entertaining by including amusing anecdotes about the ridiculously paradoxical measures of contemporary economic policy. I feel certain that this will be appreciated by the serious reader.

Some people may object that it is insufficient to discuss these problems from an economic standpoint only. They include, it is said, more than merely economic aspects, namely, politics, philosophy of life, and moral values. I definitely disagree. All political arguments of our time center around capitalism, socialism, and interventionism. Certainly there are many more things in life. But our contemporaries—not just the economists—have placed the question of economic organization in the center of their political thinking. All political parties confine themselves to economic aspects; they recommend their programs with the assertion that their execution will make their supporters richer. All pressure groups fight for economic betterment; all parties are today economic parties. Hitler and Mussolini proclaim: "We 'have-nots' are out to get a share of the wealth of the plutocrats." Ownership is the battle cry of the day. We may well approve or disapprove of this fact, but we cannot deny its existence.

Therefore it is not arrogance or narrow mindedness that leads the economist to discuss these things from the standpoint of economics. No one who is not able to form an independent opinion about the admittedly difficult and highly technical problem of calculation in the socialist economy should take sides in the question of socialism versus capitalism. No one should speak about interventionism who has not examined the economic consequences of interventionism. An end should be put to the common practice of discussing these problems from the standpoint of the prevailing errors, fallacies, and prejudices. It might be more entertaining to avoid the real issues and merely to use popular catchwords and emotional slogans. But politics is a serious matter. Those who do not want to think its problems through to the end should keep away from it.

The moment has come in which our contemporaries have thoroughly to reconsider their political ideas. Every thinking person has frankly to admit that the two doctrines which for the past twenty years have exclusively dominated the political scene have obviously failed. Both anti-fascism and anti-communism have utterly lost their meaning since Hitler and Stalin have ceased to conceal their alliance from the world.[2]

I hope to render with this book a service to those who seek a clarification of their ideas and a better understanding of the problems of the world today.

2. I predicted the cooperation between the Nazis and Bolsheviks as early as 1925 in my article "Anti-Marxism" (*Weltwirtschaftliches Archiv*, Vol. 21, p. 279) reprinted in my 1929 book *Kritik des Interventionismus*, p. 106. [English translation, Arlington House, 1977, p. 122; 2nd English edition, Foundation for Economic Education, 1996, pp. 81–82. When this book was written Germany and the U.S.S.R. were allies, united through a non-aggression treaty which lasted only from August 1939 until June 22, 1941, when the Germans attacked Russia without warning.—Editor]

I do not want to close this preface without expressing my sincere gratitude to my two colleagues Drs. Heinrich Bund and Thomas McManus who have aided in the preparation of the manuscript and in its translation.

Ludwig von Mises
November 1941

 INTERVENTIONISM

Introduction

1. The Problem

We call capitalism or market economy that form of social cooperation which is based on private ownership of the means of production.

Socialism, communism, or planned economy, on the other hand, is the form of social cooperation which is based on public ownership of the means of production. The terms state capitalism and authoritarian economy have essentially the same meaning.

It is frequently asserted that a third form of social cooperation is feasible as a permanent form of economic organization, namely a system of private ownership of the means of production in which the government intervenes, by orders and prohibitions, in the exercise of ownership. This third system is called interventionism. All governments which do not openly profess socialism tend to be interventionist nowadays, and all political parties recommend at least some degree of interventionism.[1] It is claimed that this system of interventionism is as far from socialism as it is from capitalism, that as a third solution to the social problem it stands midway between the two systems, and that while retaining the advantages of both it avoids the disadvantages inherent in both.

In this study the question will be analyzed whether we are justified in considering interventionism as a possible and viable system of social cooperation. We shall attempt to answer the question whether interventionism is able to accomplish what its advocates expect, and whether, perhaps, it does not produce consequences diametrically opposed to those sought by its application.

---

1. The orthodox Marxists, however, recommend interventionism in full recognition of the fact that it paralyzes and destroys the capitalistic market economy and, thus, in their opinion, leads to socialism. This was the argument advanced as long as a century ago by Friedrich Engels.

Such an analysis has more than merely academic value. With the exception of the two socialist countries of Soviet Russia and Nazi Germany, interventionism is today throughout the world the prevailing economic system. Therefore, an understanding of interventionism and its inevitable consequences is an essential prerequisite for a comprehension of present-day economic problems.

We intend in this analysis to refrain from value judgments. Consequently we do not ask whether interventionism is good or bad, moral or immoral, to be commended or condemned. We merely ask from the standpoint of those who want to put it into operation whether it serves or frustrates their intentions. In other words, does its application attain the ends sought?

In order to answer these questions we have first to clarify the meaning of the terms of capitalism, socialism, government, and intervention.

2. Capitalism or Market Economy

In the capitalistic economy the means of production are owned by individuals or associations of individuals, such as corporations. The owners use the means of production directly to produce, or they lend them, for a compensation, to others who want to use them in production. The individuals or associations of individuals who produce with their own or with borrowed money are called entrepreneurs.

Superficially, it seems that the entrepreneurs decide what should be produced, and how it should be produced. However, as they do not produce for their own needs but for those of all members of the community, they have to sell the products on the market to consumers, that is, those individuals who want to use and consume them. Only that entrepreneur is successful and realizes a profit who knows how to produce in the best and cheapest way, that is with a minimum expenditure of material and labor, the articles most urgently wanted by the consumers. Therefore, in actuality the consumers, not the entrepreneurs, determine the direction and scope of production. In the market economy the consumers are sovereign. They are the masters, and the entrepreneurs have to strive, in their own interest, to serve the wishes of the consumers to the best of their ability.

The market economy has been called a democracy of consumers, because it brings about a daily recurring ballot of consumer preferences. The casting of votes at an election and the spending of dollars in the market are both methods of expressing public opinion. The consumers decide, by buying or by refraining from buying, the success or failure of the entrepreneurs. They make poor entrepreneurs rich and rich entrepreneurs poor. They take away the means of production from those entrepreneurs who do not know how to use them best in the service of the consumers and transfer them to those who know how to make better use of them. It is true that only the entrepreneurs producing consumers' goods have direct contact with the consumers; only they are immediately dependent on the consumers; only they receive directly the consumers' orders. But they transmit those orders and their dependence to the entrepreneurs who bring producers' goods to the market. The producers of consumers' goods have to purchase where they can, at lowest cost, the producers' goods which are required for the ultimate satisfaction of the wants of the consumers. Should they fail to use the cheapest supplies, should they fail to make the most efficient use of the producers' goods in production, they would be unable to satisfy the wants of the consumers at lowest prices; more efficient entrepreneurs who know better how to buy and how to produce would crowd them out of the market. The consumer as buyer may follow his own liking and his own fancy. The entrepreneur must do the buying for his enterprise as the most efficient satisfaction of the wants of the consumers dictates. Deviations from this line prescribed by the consumers affect the entrepreneur's returns, thus causing losses and endangering his position as entrepreneur.

Such is the oft-decried harshness of the entrepreneur who figures everything in dollars and cents. He is forced to take this attitude by order of the consumers, who are unwilling to reimburse the entrepreneurs for unnecessary expenditures. What in everyday language is called economy is simply law prescribed by the consumers for the actions of the entrepreneurs and their helpers. The consumers, by their behavior in the market, are the ones who indirectly determine prices and wages and, thus, the distribution of wealth among the members of society. Their choices in the market determine who shall be entrepreneur and owner of the means of production. By every dollar spent, the consumers influence the direction, size, and kind of production and marketing.

The entrepreneurs do not form a closed class or order. Any individual may become an entrepreneur if he has the ability to foresee the future development of the market better than his fellow-citizens, if he can inspire the confidence of capitalists, and if his attempts to act on his own risk and responsibility prove successful. One becomes an entrepreneur, literally, by pushing forward and exposing oneself to the impartial test to which the market puts everyone who wants to become or remain an entrepreneur. Everyone has the privilege of choosing whether he wants to submit himself to this rigorous examination or not. He doesn't have to wait to be asked to do so—he must step forward on his own initiative, and he has to worry where and how he can secure the means for his entrepreneurial activity.

For decades it was repeatedly asserted that the rise of poor people into entrepreneurial positions was no longer possible in the stage of "late capitalism." The proof for this assertion was never given. Since this thesis was first voiced, the composition of the entrepreneurial class has basically changed; a considerable part of the former entrepreneurs and their heirs have disappeared, and the most outstanding entrepreneurs of today are again what we usually call self-made men. This constant recomposition of the entrepreneurial elite is as old as the capitalist economy itself and forms an integral part of it.

What is true of the entrepreneurs holds true for the capitalists as well. Only the capitalist who knows how to use his capital properly (from the consumer's point of view), that is, to invest it so that the means of production will be employed most efficiently in the service of consumers, is able to keep and augment his property. If he does not want to suffer losses the capitalist has to place his means at the disposal of successful enterprises. In the market economy the capitalist, just like the entrepreneurs and the workers, serves the consumers. It seems superfluous to point out specifically in this connection that the consumers are not merely consumers but that the totality of the consumers is identical with the totality of the workers, entrepreneurs, and capitalists.

In a world of unchanging economic conditions the exact amounts which the entrepreneurs would expend for the means of production as wages, interest, and rent would later be received by them in the prices of their products. Production costs would thus equal the prices of the products and the entrepreneurs would neither make profits nor suffer losses. But the world of reality is constantly changing, and therefore all industrial activity is essentially uncertain and speculative in character. Goods are produced to meet a future demand, about which we have little positive knowledge in the present. It is from this uncertainty that profits and losses arise; the profits and losses of the entrepreneurs

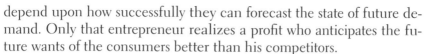

depend upon how successfully they can forecast the state of future demand. Only that entrepreneur realizes a profit who anticipates the future wants of the consumers better than his competitors.

It is irrelevant to the entrepreneur, as the servant of the consumers, whether the wishes and wants of the consumers are wise or unwise, moral or immoral. He produces what the consumers want. In this sense he is amoral. He manufactures whiskey and guns just as he produces food and clothing. It is not his task to teach reason to the sovereign consumers. Should one entrepreneur, for ethical reasons of his own, refuse to manufacture whiskey, other entrepreneurs would do so as long as whiskey is wanted and bought. It is not because we have distilleries that people drink whiskey; it is because people like to drink whiskey that we have distilleries. One may deplore this. But it is not up to the entrepreneurs to improve mankind morally. And they are not to be blamed if those whose duty this is have failed to do so.

Thus the market in the capitalist economy is the process regulating production and consumption. It is the nerve center of the capitalist system. Through it the orders of the consumers are transmitted to the producers, and the smooth functioning of the economic system is secured thereby. The market prices establish themselves at the level which equates demand and supply. When, other things being equal, more goods are brought to the market, prices fall; when, other things being equal, demand increases, prices rise.

One thing more must be noted. If within a society based on private ownership of the means of production some of these means are publicly owned and operated, this still does not make for a mixed system which would combine socialism and private property. As long as only certain individual enterprises are publicly owned, the remaining being privately owned, the characteristics of the market economy which determine economic activity remain essentially unimpaired. The publicly owned enterprises, too, as buyers of raw materials, semi-finished goods, and labor, and as sellers of goods and services, must fit into the mechanism of the market economy; they are subject to the same laws of the market. In order to maintain their position they, too, have to strive after profits or at least to avoid losses. When it is attempted to mitigate or eliminate this dependence by covering the losses of such enterprises by subsidies out of public funds, the only accomplishment is a shifting of this dependence somewhere else. This is because the means for the subsidies have to be raised somewhere. They may be raised by collecting taxes; the burden of such taxes has its effects on the market, not on the government collecting the tax; it is the market and not the revenue department which decides upon whom the tax falls and how it affects production and consumption. In these facts the domination of the market and the inescapable force of its laws are evidenced.[2]

3. The Socialist Economy

In the socialist order all means of production are owned by the nation. The government decides what should be produced and how it should be produced and allots each individual a share of the consumers' goods for his consumption.

This system might be realized according to two different patterns.

The one pattern—we may call it the Marxian or Russian pattern—is purely bureaucratic. All economic enterprises are departments of the government just as are the administrations of the army and the navy or the postal system. Every single plant, shop, or farm stands in the same relation to the superior central organization as does a post office to the postal system. The whole nation forms one single labor army with compulsory service; the commander of this army is the chief of state.

The second pattern—we may call it the German system—differs from the first one in that it, seemingly and nominally, maintains private ownership of the means of production, entrepreneurship, and market exchange. Entrepreneurs do the buying and selling, pay the workers, contract debts, and pay interest and amortization. But they are entrepreneurs in name only. The government tells these seeming entrepreneurs what and how to produce, at what prices, and from whom to buy, at what prices, and to whom to sell. The government decrees to whom and under what terms the capitalists should entrust their funds and where and at what wages laborers should work. Market exchange is but a sham. As all prices, wages, and interest rates are being fixed by the authority, they are prices, wages, and interest rates in appearance only; in reality they are merely determinations of quantity relations in authoritarian orders. The authority, not the consumers, directs produc-

2. For a fuller discussion of this point, I have to refer to what is said in my book, *Nationalökonomie, Theorie des Handelns und Wirtschaftens* (Geneva, 1940), pp. 224–228. [See Mises's *Human Action*, the English-language successor to *Nationalökonomie*, pp. 233–235 in first 1949 ed.; pp. 232–234 in later editions.—Editor]

tion. This is socialism with the outward appearance of capitalism. The labels of the capitalistic market economy are retained, but they signify here something entirely different from what they mean in the true market economy.

We have to point out this possibility to prevent a confusion of socialism and interventionism. The system of a hampered market economy or interventionism differs from socialism by the very fact that it is still a market economy. The authority seeks to influence the market by the intervention of its coercive power, but it does not want to eliminate the market completely. It desires that production and consumption should develop along lines different from those prescribed by the unhindered market, and it wants to achieve this aim by injecting into the workings of the market, orders, commands, and prohibitions, for whose enforcement the power and constraint apparatus stand ready. But these are isolated interventions; they do not combine into a completely integrated system which regulates all prices, wages, and interest rates, and which thus places the direction of production and consumption in the hands of the authority.

It is not the task of this essay to raise the question whether a socialist economy is feasible. The subject matter of our analysis is interventionism, not socialism. Consequently, it is only incidentally that we point out that socialism is unworkable as a universal economic system, because a socialist society would not be able to make rational calculations in economic matters. The economic calculation which we use in the capitalistic economy is based on market prices, which are formed in the market for all goods and services, consequently for producers' goods and for labor services as well. Only money prices make it possible to bring costs which originate through the expenditure of various goods and different qualities of labor to a common denominator so they may be compared with prices which were realized or which can be realized on the market. Thus it is possible to establish, in definite figures, the probable effect of a planned action and to know the actual effect of actions carried out in the past. In a socialist economy which does not have prices for producers' goods—there being no market for the means of production because they are all owned by the state—the opportunity to make such calculations would not exist.

Let us assume, for instance, that the government of a socialist country would want to build a house. The house may be built of brick or wood, stone, concrete, or steel. Each of these ways offers, as seen from the point of view of the evaluating government, various advantages, requires different expenditures of labor and materials, and requires a different production period. On which method will the government decide? It cannot reduce the different expenditures of labor and materials of various kinds to a common denominator and, therefore, cannot compare them. It cannot make either the construction period or the use period play a calculable part in its considerations. Therefore it cannot compare expenditures and benefits, costs and returns. It does not know whether or not its decisions concerning its use of the factors of production are rational from the standpoint of its own valuation of consumers' goods.

Around the middle of the [nineteenth] century, for example, the suggestion might have been presented to such a government to restrict sheep-rearing considerably in Europe and to find a new location for it in Australia. Or the suggestion might have been made to replace horse power with steam power. What means did the government have at its disposal to ascertain whether these and other innovations were advantageous from an economic standpoint?

Yes, say the socialists, but capitalistic calculation is not infallible either; the capitalist too may err. Certainly, this has happened before and will happen again, because all economic activity looks toward the future, and the future is always unknown. All plans become futile when the expectations with regard to future developments are not fulfilled. But this objection is beside the point. Today, we calculate from the standpoint of our *present* knowledge and from the standpoint of our *present* expectations about the future. The problem does not lie in the fact that the government may err because it may misjudge the future, but rather in its inability to make calculations even from the standpoint of its present valuations and expectations. If, for instance, a government proceeds with the erection of tuberculosis hospitals it may discover later, when a simpler and more efficient means of combating the disease is found, that it invested capital and labor unwisely. But the crux of the problem is: How can the government know *today* how to build such hospitals in the most economical way?

Some railways would not have been built around 1900 if one could have foreseen, at that time, the development of motor traffic and aviation. But the entrepreneur who built railways then knew which among the construction alternatives he had to choose from the standpoint of his valuations and expectations at that time, and on the basis of market prices reflecting entrepreneurial evaluations of prospective demand.

But this is exactly what the government of a socialist community will not know. It will be like the captain of a ship trying to sail the high seas without the resources of science or art of navigation.

We have presupposed that the government has decided to undertake a certain project. But even to arrive at this decision requires economic calculation. The decision in favor of building a power plant can only be made when it is established that this project would not divert means of production from more urgent uses. How shall this be ascertained without calculation?

4. The Capitalist State and the Socialist State

In a market economy the state concerns itself with the protection of the life, health, and private property of its citizens against force or fraud. The state insures the smooth working of the market economy by the weight of its coercive power. It refrains, however, from any interference with the freedom of action of the people engaged in production and distribution so long as such actions do not involve the use of force or fraud against the life, health, safety, or property of others. This very fact characterizes such a community as a market economy or a capitalist economy.

If liberals,[3] i.e., classical liberals, oppose governmental interference in the economic sphere they do so because they feel certain that the market economy is the only efficient and workable system of social co-operation. They are convinced that no other system would be in a position to bring more welfare and happiness to the people. The English and French liberals and the fathers of the U.S. Constitution insisted upon the protection of private property, not to further the selfish interests of one class, but rather for the protection of the whole people and because they saw the welfare of the nation and of each individual most secure in the system of a market economy.

It is, therefore, naive to say that the true liberal advocates of private property are enemies of the state because they want to see the realm of governmental activity limited. They are not enemies of the state but

3. The term "liberal" is here used in the sense which generally was attributed to it in the nineteenth century. In the Anglo-Saxon countries "liberal" has come to mean the opposite of what this term used to signify in the past; today it means either radical-interventionist or even socialist. Those whom one would have in the past called liberals the American socialists and interventionists today call reactionaries, conservatives, or economic royalists. In this change of the meaning of liberalism, the victory of interventionist ideas and the abandonment of a market economy are clearly evidenced. The old liberalism has even lost its name.

opponents of both socialism and interventionism because they believe in the superior efficacy of the market economy. They want a strong and well-administered state because they assign to it an important task: the protection of the system of a market economy.

Even more naive were the Prussian metaphysicians when they maintained that the program of the adherents of a market economy was negative. To these supporters of Prussian totalitarianism everything seemed negative that stood in the way of their desire to create more governmental jobs. The program of the advocates of a market economy is negative only in the sense in which every program is negative: It excludes all other programs. Because the true liberals are positively for private ownership of the means of production and for a market economy they are necessarily against socialism and interventionism.

Under socialism all economic matters are the responsibility of the state. The government gives orders in all lines of production just as in the army or in the navy. There is no sphere of private activity; everything is directed by the government. The individual is like the inmate of an orphanage or of a penitentiary. He has to do the work which he is ordered to do and he can consume only what has been allotted to him by the government. He can read only those books and papers printed by the government printing office and he can travel only if the government grants him the means for doing so. He has to assume the occupation which the government has chosen for him and he has to change his occupation and his domicile when the government commands. In this sense, we may say that the citizens of a socialist community are not free.[4]

5. The Interventionist State

Under the system of a hampered market economy or interventionism both government and entrepreneurs are distinctly separate factors functioning in the economic sphere. The dualism of market and authority exists also in the system of a hampered market exchange. In contrast to the system of a pure market economy, however, the authority does not confine itself to the prevention of disturbances of market exchange. The government itself interferes by isolated interventions in the workings of the market; it orders and it forbids.

---

4. "Freedom," say the Prussian metaphysicians, "is merely a negative concept." "Freedom," said Lenin, "is a bourgeois prejudice."

The intervention is an isolated order by the authority in command of the social power apparatus; it forces the entrepreneur and the owner of the means of production to use these means in a way different from what they would do under the pressure of the market. The order may be by command or interdiction. Command and interdiction need not ostensibly emanate from the government. It may happen that commands and interdictions emanate from a different source and that this other agency also supplies the power apparatus to enforce its orders. If the authority condones this procedure or even supports it, then the situation is the same as that created by direct governmental orders. If the government does not want to consent and opposes this action with its power apparatus, but without avail, this is evidence that another authority has succeeded in establishing itself and in contesting governmental supremacy.

Undoubtedly the government has the power to issue such commands and interdictions and also has the power to enforce them, through its police force. But the questions with which we are concerned in this essay are: Do these measures enable the government to achieve the aims it seeks? Do not these interventions perhaps produce results which, from the government's point of view, appear even less desirable than the conditions in the free-market economy which it seeks to change?

Consequently, we shall not concern ourselves with the question whether the government is in the hands of able or ineffectual, noble or ignoble men.[5] Even the ablest and noblest man can achieve his aim only if he uses the proper means.

Nor do we have to deal with those interventions of the authority which are immediately aimed at consumption. The authority might, for instance, temporarily or permanently forbid the consumer to eat certain foods—let us say for health or religious reasons. The authority thus assumes the role of a guardian of the individual. It deems the individual incapable of looking out for his own best interests; he is to be protected by his paternal overseer from suffering harm.

The question whether the authority should pursue such a course or not is a political question, not an economic one. If one believes that the

---

5. Hegel called the state "the Absolute." Ferdinand Lassalle said "the State is God." Professor Werner Sombart, in his book *German Socialism*, which is a bestseller in the Third Reich and has been translated into English as well as French, declares that the "Führer" receives his orders from God. We do not want to contradict the sayings of such great men; we merely point out that they have nothing to do with the subject matter of our analysis.

authority is God-given and is called upon to play the part of Providence to the individual, or if one thinks that the authority has to represent the interests of society against the conflicting interests of the egoistic individuals, one will find this attitude justified. If the authority is wiser than its subjects with their limited intelligence, if it knows better what furthers the happiness of the individual than he himself pretends to know, or if the authority feels called upon to sacrifice the welfare of the individual to the well-being of the whole, then it should not hesitate to set the aims for the actions of the individuals.

It would be an error, of course, to believe that the guardianship of the authority over the individual could remain confined to the domain of health, that the authority would conceivably be satisfied to forbid or to limit the use of dangerous poisons like opium, morphine, possibly also alcohol and nicotine, but that otherwise the freedom of the individual would remain untouched. Once the principle is acknowledged that the consumption choices of the individual are to be supervised and restricted by the authority, how far this control will expand depends only on the authority and the public opinion which motivates it. It then becomes logically impossible to oppose tendencies which want to subject all activity of the individual to the care of the state. Why only protect the body from the harm caused by poisons or drugs? Why not also protect our minds and souls from dangerous doctrines and opinions imperiling our eternal salvation? Depriving the individual of the freedom of the choice of consumption logically leads to the abolition of all freedom.

We may now turn to the economic side of the problem. When economics deals with the problems of interventionism it has only those measures in mind which primarily affect the means and not the aims of action. And it does not have any other standard by which to judge these measures than the one whether they are or are not able to achieve the aims which the authority seeks. The fact that the authority is in a position to restrict the choice of consumption for the individual and thus to alter the data of the market is beyond the scope of economic discussion.

For these reasons we do not concern ourselves with authoritarian measures immediately aimed at the direction of consumption which actually attain this aim without affecting other fields as well. We accept the action of the consumers in the market and do not take into consideration to what extent, if any, this action is influenced by the authority. We accept the valuations and the demands of the consumers as a fact, and we do not ask whether the consumers buy gas masks on their own initiative or because the government ordered them to do so, nor whether they buy less alcohol because they prefer other goods or because the government penalizes intoxication. Our task, however, is to analyze those interventions of the authority which are directed not at the consumers but at the owners of the means of production and at the entrepreneurs. And we do not ask whether these interventions are justified nor whether they conform to our wishes or to the wishes of the consumers. We merely inquire whether these measures can achieve the aims which the government wishes to attain.

6. The Plea for Moral Reform

Before we proceed, however, it appears advisable to give consideration to a doctrine which deserves some attention, if for no other reason than because it is backed by some of our most distinguished contemporaries.

We refer to the belief that it does not require the intervention of the government to bring the market economy to ways other than those it takes when it is able to develop unhampered. Christian social reformers and some representatives of an ethically motivated social reform think the religious and moral conscience ought to guide the "good" person in the economic realm as well. If all entrepreneurs would watch not only their profit and their selfish individual interests but would always think also of their religious and social obligations, the orders of the government would not be necessary to bring things into the proper channels. Not reform of the state would be required, but rather a moral purification of mankind, a return to God and to the moral law, an abandonment of the vices of selfishness and egoism. Then, it would not be difficult to bring private property of the means of production in accord with the social welfare. One would have freed the economy of the pernicious consequences of capitalism without having restricted, by governmental intervention, the freedom and initiative of the individual. One would have destroyed the Moloch Capitalism without having it replaced with the Moloch State.

We do not have to deal here with the value judgments underlying this doctrine. What these critics find objectionable in capitalism is irrelevant, and the errors and misunderstandings they expound need not concern us. We are only interested in their suggestion to build a social order on the dual foundation of private ownership of the means of production and of a moral law delimiting the exercise of this property right. This ideal social order supposedly is not socialism because under it the individuals, particularly the entrepreneurs, capitalists, and proprietors, are no longer guided by the profit motive, but by their consciences. Nor is it supposed to be interventionism, because it does not require governmental interventions to secure the working of the economic machine.

In the market economy the individual is free in his actions as far as private property and the market extend. Here, only *his* valuations count. Whatever he may choose, the choice he makes prevails. His action is, for the other parties in the market, a fact which they have to take into account. The consequences of his action in the market are reflected in profits or losses; they are the one cog fitting his activity into the machinery of social cooperation. Society does not tell the individual what to do and what not to do; nobody gives orders and demands obedience, no force is used unless for the protection of private property and of the market against violence. The cooperation is the result of the workings of the market. Those who do not fit themselves to the best of their ability into the social cooperation feel the consequences of their rebellion, their negligence, their errors and mistakes. This coordination does not require anything more from the individual than acting in his own interest. Therefore, there is no need of orders from an authority telling the individual what to do and what not to do, and there is no need of a power instrument to enforce such orders.

Beyond the realm of private property and market exchange lies the realm of unlawful actions; there society has erected barriers for the protection of private property and of the market against force, fraud, and malice. Here freedom no longer reigns, but compulsion. Here, not everything is permitted, here a line is drawn between the lawful and the unlawful. Here the police power is ready to intervene. If it were any different every individual would be free to break through the barriers of the legal order.

The reformers whose suggestions we are here discussing want to establish additional ethical norms besides the legal order and the moral code designed to maintain and to protect private property. They desire results in production and consumption different from those produced by the unhampered market in which there is no limitation upon the individuals save the one not to violate private property. They want to eliminate the forces which guide the actions of the individual in the market economy. They call them selfishness, egoism, the profit motive, or the like, and they want to replace them with other forces. They speak of conscience, of altruism, of awe of God, of brotherly love. And they want to replace "production for profit" with "production for use." They believe that this would suffice to secure the harmonious cooperation of men in an economy based on the division of labor so that there would not be any need for interventions—commands and interdictions—by an authority.

The error inherent in this doctrine is that it fails to recognize the important part the forces which it condemns as immoral play in the workings of the market. Precisely because the market economy does not demand anything from the individual with regard to the use of the means of production; precisely because he does not have to do anything not in his own interest; precisely because the market economy accepts him as he is; and precisely because his "egoism" is sufficient to coordinate him to the whole of social cooperation, his activity does not need the direction of norms nor of authorities enforcing the adherence to these norms. If the individual looks out for his own interest within the framework provided by private property and market exchange he is doing everything the society expects of him. In following the profit motive his action necessarily becomes social.

By trying to replace the profit motive, the guiding principle of private ownership of the means of production, by so-called moral motives, we are destroying the purposiveness and the efficiency of the market economy. Simply by advising the individual to follow the voice of his conscience and to replace egoism by altruism we cannot create a reasonable social order which could supplant the market economy. It is not enough to suggest that the individual should not buy at the lowest price and should not sell at the highest price. It would be necessary to go further and to establish rules of conduct which would guide the individual in his activity.

The reformer thinks, for instance, the entrepreneur is hard and selfish when he uses his superiority to undersell his less efficient competitor and thus forces him to give up his entrepreneurial position. But just what is the "altruistic" entrepreneur to do? Shall he never sell at prices below those of any one of his competitors? Or shall he, under certain conditions, have the right to undersell competitors?

The reformer thinks also: The entrepreneur is hard and selfish when he takes advantage of market conditions and refuses to sell the goods cheaply enough to make them available to the poor who cannot afford them at the prevailing high price. What is the "good" entrepreneur supposed to do? Shall he give the goods away? As long as he asks *any* price for them, no matter how low, *there will always be a demand which will not be satisfied*. Which potential buyers is the entrepreneur entitled to exclude from the acquisition of the goods by insisting on a certain price?

We do not have to analyze here in detail the consequences of a deviation from the market price. If the seller is not permitted to undersell his less efficient competitors at least a part of the supply will not be sold. If, in the interest of the poor, he is supposed to sell below the market his stock will not be sufficient to satisfy all those who are willing to pay his low price. We shall have more to say on this matter in our analysis of interferences with the price structure.[6] Here, we merely wish to emphasize that it is not enough simply to tell the entrepreneur that he should not be guided by the market. We would have to tell him what to do. We would have to tell him how far to go in his price concessions and price demands. If the profit motive will no longer determine what and in what quantities he is to produce we shall have to give him definite orders which he will have to obey. This means that his activity must be guided by the very type of authoritarian orders which the reformers tried to make superfluous by appealing to conscience, morality, and brotherly love.

When we speak of "just" prices and "fair" wages we have to keep in mind that the only standard by which we can measure the justice and fairness of prices and wages is their compatibility with an ideal social order. If this ideal social order is sought outside of the market economy, then it cannot be realized by merely exhorting the individual to be "just" in his actions. It is necessary to specify what is just or unjust in each instance. Furthermore, rules must be established exactly regulating all possible cases, and an agency must be authorized to interpret these norms authentically, to enforce them, and also to supplement and modify them whenever necessary. It is irrelevant whether this authority is the worldly state or a theocratic priesthood.

Reformers address their plea for the abandonment of egoism in fa-

---

6. Cf. below, chapter II, section 2.

vor of altruism to the entrepreneurs and proprietors, sometimes to the workers. But the decisive factors in a market economy are the consumers. They determine the attitudes the entrepreneurs and proprietors take. Therefore this plea should be addressed to the consumers. The reformers would have to make the consumer renounce the better and cheaper goods so as to protect less efficient producers. The consumers would have to boycott those goods the sale of which endangers the continuance of conditions which appear socially desirable. And the consumers would have to impose upon themselves restrictions in their buying so as to make it possible for their less wealthy fellow citizens to purchase. If the reformers expect this attitude from the consumer, then they would have to tell him just how, where, and what he should buy, and at what prices. In addition they would have to take measures to force the consumer who does not follow these instructions to obey. But then the reformers would have done precisely what they wanted to avoid, namely, they would have regulated the economy by definite orders and would have penalized the disobedience of such orders.

I.

Interference by Restriction

1. The Nature of Restrictive Measures

Restrictive measures are those measures undertaken by the authority which directly and primarily are intended to divert production, in the widest meaning of the word, including commerce and transportation, from the ways which it would take in the unhampered economy. Each interference diverts production from the channels prescribed by the market. The peculiar characteristic of restrictive measures lies in the fact that the diversion of production is a necessary and not unintended result of the intervention, and that the diversion of production is precisely what the authority seeks to accomplish by its action. Each intervention has also the necessary effect of diverting consumption from the ways which it would choose in the unhampered market economy. The restrictive measure is no exception in this respect. But the diversion of consumption is not the aim which its originators pursue; they want to influence production. The fact that these measures influence consumption as well seems to them a side effect which they either do not want at all or which they accept as unavoidable.

By restrictive measures the authority forbids the manufacture of certain goods, or it forbids the application of certain methods of production, or it makes manufacture by such methods more difficult and more expensive. The authority thereby eliminates some of the means available for the satisfaction of human wants. The effect of the intervention is that men find themselves in a position where they may only use their knowledge and ability, their efforts and their material resources in a less efficient way. Such measures make people poorer.

Despite all attempts to invalidate this argument, the fact remains indisputable. In the unhampered market, forces are at work which tend to put every means of production to the use in which it is most beneficial for the satisfaction of human wants. When the authority interferes with this process in order to bring about a different use of the productive factors it can only impair the supply, it cannot improve it.

This has been proved in an excellent and irrefutable manner for the most important group of restrictive measures by the extensive discussion dealing with the economic effects of barriers to international trade. It appears superfluous to add anything in this respect to the teachings of the classical school of political economy.

2. Costs and Benefits of Restrictive Measures

One might be of the opinion that the disadvantages which restrictive measures cause by diminishing productivity, and thus impairing supply, are outweighed by advantages in other fields. The authority might claim, for instance, that the preservation of a group of less efficient producers is so important that the resulting cut in consumption appears quite justified. It might consider it justified to make bread more expensive for the masses of the people so that owners of less fertile farms might earn higher returns. The authority might also consider it a postulate of wise statesmanship to prohibit the introduction of certain machines in order to protect those enterprises which cannot afford such appliances from the competition of better equipped business units. By outlawing department stores, chain stores, and similar forms of trade organizations, the authority might make it possible for the small retailers to stay in competition even though the interests of consumers suffer.

If such measures are undertaken in full recognition of their effects, if the authority is fully aware of what it is doing and what results it will accomplish, one might disapprove of its action only if one does not approve of its aim. But one cannot regard the action of the authority as contrary to purpose or senseless. From the standpoint of *its* aims and purposes, *its* action appears correct. To make the farmers better off, it wants to impose a burden on the bread consumers buy; in order to accomplish this purpose it has chosen the proper means when it imposes a protective tariff or an import prohibition on grain and flour.

We all know that these things are presented in a different light to the public. It was successfully attempted to convince public opinion that the tariff barriers do not reduce supply, but rather that they increase supply. The protection of the small craftsman against the competition of "big business," the protection of the small retailer against the competition of department and chain stores, were represented as measures for the general welfare, and as serving the protection of the consumers against exploitation. This was the only way to get favorable consideration for a political policy, the very essence of which lies in the granting of privileges and advantages to particular groups at the expense of the other groups of the community.

3. The Restrictive Measure as a Privilege

The policy of restrictive measures was believed to be a policy favoring producers, while the policy which does not want to impair the working of the market process was considered to be a policy favoring consumers. The advocates of the former policy justify it by pointing out that it was not the task of the authority to pursue a policy for the benefit of those who merely consume the products of other people's efforts; rather the authority should serve the man actively engaged in production. But in a system which is based on the division of labor, all are both producers and consumers. There are no consumers whose income would not flow from production. The consumer is either an entrepreneur, an owner of means of production, or a worker. Or he is, as a member of a family, being supported by an entrepreneur, an owner of means of production, or by a worker. Each producer, on the other hand, is necessarily also a consumer. It is naive to claim that a single measure or a single policy would protect the interests of producers against the interests of consumers. The only statement which can properly be made is that almost every restrictive measure[1] brings advantages to a limited group of people while it affects adversely all others, or at least a majority of others. The interventions, therefore, may be regarded as privileges, which are granted to some at the expense of others.

Privileges benefit the recipient and impair the position of the other members of the system. If the privileges benefit a limited number of persons only, they fulfill their purpose; they benefit them at the expense of others not so favored. If, however, all are equally benefited, then the system of privileges becomes nonsensical. As long as protective tariffs benefit only some of the producers or various groups of producers to

---

1. The limitation implied here by the word "almost" should not mean that there are restrictive measures which do not disadvantage anyone; it should indicate only that some such measures not only do not benefit anyone, but put everybody at a disadvantage.

a different extent, then some producers are still privileged. But if all producers are equally protected, then the policy becomes truly self-defeating. Then nobody gains but everybody loses.

4. Restrictive Measures as Expenditures

One might consider some restrictive measures as justified if one regards them as a part of the public spending policy rather than as measures aimed at production and supply. If for love of nature or for scientific purposes we want to preserve a piece of land in its natural state as a national park and therefore want to keep it from all productive purposes, we might expect general approval so long as we keep this plan within the limits of the public budget. We might then find it more appropriate not to place the burden of this expenditure on the owners of this land but to distribute it among all citizens by buying the land rather than expropriating it. But this is not important for our analysis. Decisive is the fact that we consider this proposition from the standpoint of expenditure, not of production.

This is the only correct viewpoint to assume with regard to restrictive measures. Restrictive measures, the only possible effect of which can be the impairment of supply, should not be considered as measures of production policy. They work for consumption but not production. Restrictive measures can never bring about economic efficiency, never a system of production of goods and the improvement of the state of supply. One might differ as to the advisability of protecting the Prussian Junkers by a tariff on grain imports against the competition of the Canadian farmers who are producing on more fertile soil. But if we advocate a tariff to protect Prussian grain producers, we are not recommending a measure in favor of the production of the supply of grain, but a measure designed to assist the owners of German land at the expense of the German grain consumers. It will never be possible to base an economic system on such assistance privileges; such measures can only be paid as expenditures from means which are otherwise procured. When Louis XIV granted a sinecure out of public revenues to one of his favorites, this act was spending; it was not economic policy. The fact that restrictive measures do not deserve a consideration different from these royal privileges is obscured by the technique of their execution. But this does not change their essential nature. Whether such an expenditure is justified or not is of no concern for economic evaluation; even the kings of the *ancien régime* did not always grant favors to unworthy men.

There are undoubtedly cases in which restrictive measures appear justified to most or all of our citizens. But all restrictive measures are fundamentally expenditures. They diminish the supply of productive means available for the supply of other goods. Consequently it would be contrary to logic to represent a market economy, which is hampered by such restrictive measures, as a separate system of social cooperation in contrast to the unhampered market economy. We have to consider the restrictive measure as spending policy, not as a means of increasing the supplies of productive goods.

Once we recognize the true nature of restrictive measures and refuse to be misled by the naive efforts to justify them as "promoting welfare" or even "promoting production," we discover that the ends sought by these measures can often be accomplished much more cheaply by direct subsidies from public funds. If we do not prevent the producers from achieving the highest possible yield from the available productive resources, we will not impair the productivity of the economy and we will be in a better position to draw from the increased wealth the means necessary for subsidizing those whom we desire to privilege.

II.

Interference by Price Control

1. The Alternative: Statutory Law versus Economic Law

Measures of price control are directed at fixing prices, wages, and interest rates at amounts different from those prevailing in the unhampered market. The authority or the group expressly or tacitly entrusted by the authority with power to control prices fixes them as maximums or minimums. The police power is used to enforce these decrees.

The aim underlying such interference with the price structure of the market is either to privilege the seller (in the case of minimum prices) or to privilege the buyer (in the case of maximum prices). The minimum price should make it possible for the seller to achieve better prices for the goods he is offering; the maximum price should enable the buyer to acquire the goods he desires at a lower price. It depends on political conditions just which group the authority will favor. At times maximum prices have been established, at times minimum prices; at times maximum wages, at times minimum wages. Only for interest rates have there been only maximums, never minimums. Political expediency has always demanded such a course.

Out of the controversies over governmental regulation of prices, wages, and interest rates, the science of political economy developed. For hundreds and even for thousands of years the authorities have attempted to influence prices through the use of their power apparatus. They have imposed the heaviest penalties on those who refused to obey their orders. Innumerable lives have been lost in this struggle. In no other field has the police force displayed more eagerness to use its power, and in no other case has the vindictiveness of the authorities found more enthusiastic support by the masses. And still all these attempts failed of their objective. The explanation which this failure has found in the philosophical, theological, political, and historical literature precisely reflects the opinion of the authorities and of the masses. It was maintained that human beings were egoistical and bad by nature and that the authority had been too weak and too reluctant to use force; what were required were hard and ruthless rulers.

Realization of the truth had its origin in the observations of the effects of such measures in a narrowly confined field of application. Among the price control measures, particular importance attaches to the attempts of the authority to impart to debased coins the same value as to coins of full metallic content, and to maintain a fixed exchange ratio between the precious metals gold and silver, and later between metallic money and depreciated paper money. The reasons which caused the failure of all such attempts were early realized and were formulated in the law named after Sir Thomas Gresham.* From these early beginnings it was still a long way to the great discoveries of the Scottish and English philosophers of the eighteenth century, that the market followed certain laws which bound all market phenomena in a necessary relation.

The discovery of the inevitable laws of the market and exchange was one of the great achievements of the human mind. It laid the cornerstone for the development of liberal sociology† and gave rise to liberalism and thus brought with it our modern culture and economy. It paved the way for the great technological achievements of our time. It was at the same time the starting point of a systematic science of human action, that is, of economics.

The pre-scientific mind distinguished between the good and the bad, the just and the unjust in human action. It believed that human behavior could be evaluated and judged by the established standards of a heteronomous moral law. It thought that human action was free in the sense of not being subject to the inherent laws of human behavior. Man should, it argued, act morally; if he acted differently God would punish him in the hereafter if not during his lifetime; man's actions do not have any other consequences. Therefore, there need be no limit to what the authority might do as long as it did not come in conflict with

---

* [Sir Thomas Gresham (1519–1579) pointed out that debasing the money led to a decline in the value of English coins and to gold's leaving the country and thus was credited with developing "Gresham's law." Also see below, p. 47.—Editor]

† [Mises uses "sociology" here to mean the science of human action. He later came to consider "sociology" inexpedient for use in that sense; in his major work, *Human Action* (1949) he used the term "praxeology" to refer to the science of human action.—Editor]

a stronger power. The sovereign authority is free in the exercise of its power provided it does not exceed the boundaries of the territory in which it is sovereign; it can accomplish everything it desires. There are physical laws which it cannot change; but in the social sphere there are no limitations on what it may do.

The science of political economy began with the realization that there is another limit for the sovereignty of those in power. The economist looks beyond the state and its power apparatus and discovers that human society is the outcome of human cooperation. He discovers that there prevail laws in the realm of social cooperation which the state is unable to modify. He recognizes that the process of the market, which is the result of these laws, determines prices and that the system of market prices provides the rationale of human cooperation. Prices no longer appear as the result of an arbitrary attitude of individuals dependent on their sense of justice but are recognized as the necessary and unequivocal product of the play of market forces. Each specific constellation of data produces a specific price structure as its necessary corollary. It is not possible to change these prices—the "natural" prices—without having previously changed the data. Every deviation from the "natural" price releases forces which tend to bring the price back to its "natural" position.

This opinion is directly contrary to the belief that the authority can alter prices at will through its orders, interdictions, and penalties. If prices are determined by the structure of data, if they are the element in the process which effects social cooperation and which subordinates the activities of all individuals to the satisfaction of the wants of all members of the community, then an arbitrary change of prices, that is one independent of changes in the data, must necessarily create a disturbance in social cooperation. It is true that a strong and determined government can issue price orders and can cruelly revenge itself on those who fail to obey. But it will not achieve the aim it seeks through the price orders. Its intervention is but one of the data in the market which produces certain effects according to the inevitable laws of the market. It is extremely doubtful whether the government will be pleased with these effects and it is extremely doubtful whether the government will not consider them, when they appear, as even less desirable than the conditions it sought to change. At any rate these measures do not achieve what the authority wants to accomplish. Price interventions are, therefore, from the standpoint of the initiating authority not only ineffective and useless, but also contrary to purpose, harmful, and thus illogical.

Anyone attempting to refute the logic of these conclusions denies the possibility of analysis in the field of economics. There would otherwise be no such thing as economics and everything that has been written on economic matters would be meaningless. If prices can be fixed by the authority without producing a reaction in the market which is contrary to the intentions of the authority, then it is futile to attempt an explanation of prices on the basis of market forces. The very essence of such an explanation of market forces lies in the assumption that each constellation of the market has a corresponding price structure and that forces operate in the market which tend to restore this—"natural"—structure of prices if it is disturbed.

In their defense of price controls, the representatives of the Historical School of Political Economy, and nowadays the Institutionalists, reason quite logically from their viewpoint because they do not recognize economic theory. To them economics is merely an aggregate of authoritarian orders and measures. Illogical, however, is the argument of those who on the one hand study the problems of the market with the methods of theoretical analysis but on the other hand refuse to admit that price control measures necessarily produce results contrary to purpose.

The only alternatives are statutory law or economic law. Prices are either arbitrarily determined by the individuals in the market and may, therefore, be channeled by orders of the authorities in any desired direction; or prices are determined by the market forces commonly called supply and demand and the intervention of the authority affects the market as but one of many factors. There is no compromise possible between these two viewpoints.

2. The Reaction of the Market

Price control measures paralyze the working of the market. They destroy the market. They deprive the market economy of its steering power and render it unworkable.

The price structure of the market is characterized by its tendency to bring supply and demand into balance. If the authority attempts to fix a price different from the market price, this situation cannot prevail. In the case of maximum prices, there are potential buyers who cannot buy although they are ready to pay the price fixed by the authority, or even to pay a higher price. Or there are—in the case of minimum prices—potential sellers who cannot find buyers even though they are willing to sell at the price established by the authority, or even to sell at a lower price. The price is no longer the means of segregating those potential buyers and sellers who may buy or sell from those who may not. A different principle of selection has to come into operation. It may be that only those who come first or those who occupy a privileged position due to particular circumstances (personal connections, for instance) will actually buy or sell. But it may also be that the authority itself takes over the regulation of distribution. At any rate the market is no longer able to provide for the distribution of the available supply to the consumers. If chaotic conditions are to be avoided, and if neither chance nor force is to be relied upon to determine distribution, the authority has to undertake this task by some system of rationing.

But the market is not only engaged in the distribution of a given stock of ready consumption goods. Its foremost task consists in directing production. It directs the means of production to those uses which serve most urgent needs. If maximum prices are set below the ideal market price for certain consumers' goods only, without at the same time regulating the prices of all complementary means of production as well, then those means of production which are not completely specialized will be used to a greater extent in the production of other consumption goods which are not hit by the price fixing. Production will thus be diverted from goods which are more urgently needed by the consumer but which are affected by the price fixing, and it will go into the production of other goods which from the standpoint of the consumer are less important but which are free from regulations. If it was the intention of the authorities to make the goods covered by the price fixing more easily available by its maximum prices, then its measure failed. Its production would either be restricted or would cease completely. A simultaneous price fixing for complementary goods would not have much of an effect either, unless all complementary goods are of such specialized character that they could be used only for the production of this one good. As labor does not have this highly specialized character we may omit it from our considerations. If the authority is not willing to accept the fact that the result of its measures to make a good cheaper is that the supply of such goods stops completely, then the authority cannot confine itself to such interventions as affect merely the prices of all goods and services necessary for such production. It has to go farther and prevent capital, labor, and entrepreneurial activity from leaving this line of production. It must fix the prices of all goods and services and of interest rates also. And it must issue specific orders stating what and how goods and services should be produced and at what prices and to whom they should be sold.

The isolated price control measure fails to accomplish the purpose in the operation of the market economy which its originators aim at; it is—from the standpoint of its originators—not only useless, but also contrary to purpose because it aggravates the "evil" which it is intended to alleviate. Before the price control was instituted the good was, in the opinion of the authority, too expensive; now, it disappears from the market. But, this effect was not intended by the authority which wanted only to make the good cheaper for the consumer. On the contrary, from its standpoint we have to regard the lack of the good, its unavailability, as the greater evil; the authority aimed at an increased supply, not at a diminution of supply. We may say, therefore, that the isolated price control measure defeats its own purpose, and that a system of economic policy which is based on such measures is contrary to purpose and futile.

If the authority is not willing to remedy the evils created by such isolated intervention, by cancelling the price control measure, then it has to follow up this first step with further measures. Further orders must be added to the initial order not to demand higher prices than those decreed—the order to sell the whole supply, instructions to whom to sell and in what quantities these sales are to be made, price control measures regarding complementary goods,[1] wage rates and compulsory labor for workers, and interest rate control, and finally orders to produce and instructions about the choice of investment opportunities for the owners of the means of production. These regulations cannot be restricted to one or several branches of production only, but have to be expanded to cover all production. They must of necessity regulate the prices of all commodities, all wages, and the actions of all entrepreneurs, capitalists, landowners, and workers. But this means that

---

1. Direct fixing of prices for the material means of production which cannot be used in direct consumption may be omitted; if the prices are fixed for all consumers' goods, and if interest and wage rates are fixed, and if all workers are forced to work, and all owners of the means of production are forced to produce, then the prices of material means of production are indirectly fixed as well.

the direction of all production and distribution is placed in the hands of the authority. The market economy, whether intended or not, has turned into a socialist economy.

There are only two situations in which price control measures may be used effectively in a narrowly confined sphere:

1. Price control measures lead to a restriction of production because they make it impossible for the marginal producer to produce without a loss. The nonspecialized productive factors are being transferred to other branches of production. The highly specialized productive factors, which under market prices were used to the extent permitted by opportunities for alternative uses of the nonspecialized complementary factors, will now be used to a smaller extent; a part of them will not be employed. But if the quantity of highly specialized factors is so limited that they are completely utilized under the rule of market prices for the products, then there is a certain field of latitude given for authoritarian orders which lower prices. The price fixing does not cause a restriction of production as long as it does not absorb completely the absolute rent of the marginal producers. An intervention which does not go beyond this limit does not decrease supply. But as it increases demand it creates maladjustments between supply and demand which lead to chaotic conditions unless the authority itself provides for the allocation of the products among prospective buyers.

As an example: The authority must establish maximum rents for apartments and for store space in central urban locations. If the authority does not go as far as to make agricultural utilization of the land appear preferable to the owners, this action will not decrease the supply of apartments and stores.[2] But, at the prices fixed by the authority the demand will exceed the available facilities. How the authority distributes these limited facilities among those who are willing to pay the fixed rent is immaterial. No matter what the distribution, the result will be that a return is taken from the landowner and given to the tenants. The authority has taken wealth from some individuals and given it to others.

2. The second situation in which price control measures can be used with some degree of effectiveness is offered by the case of monopoly prices. The price control measure may succeed in the case of monopoly prices if it does not intend to lower the prices below the point at

---

2. For the sake of simplification we disregard construction costs.

which the competitive price would be in the nonmonopolized, unhampered market. In the case of monopoly prices established by an international cartel of mercury producers, a world (or international) authority may successfully enforce price controls which will bring the price of mercury down to the point at which it would sell under competition among several producers. Of course, the same holds true in the case of institutional monopolies. If an intervention by the authorities has created the necessary conditions for monopoly prices, then a second decree may again destroy them. If by the grant of a patent right an inventor was placed in a position to demand monopoly prices then the authority may also take away the previously granted privilege by fixing a price for the patented article which would otherwise be possible only under competition. Thus, price fixing was effective in the time of the guilds which aimed at monopoly prices. Thus it may also be effective against cartels made possible by protective tariffs.

Authorities like to appraise the effects of their actions optimistically. If the price fixing has the effect that goods of inferior quality take the place of better quality merchandise, the authority is only too ready to disregard the difference in the quality and to persist in the illusion that its intervention has had the effect it desired. At times and temporarily a small but very dearly bought success may be achieved. The producers of goods hit by the price fixing may prefer to bear losses for a certain time rather than to run new risks; they may be afraid, for instance, that their plants will be looted by the incited masses without adequate protection of the government being available. In such instances the price control measure leads to the consumption of capital and thus indirectly and eventually to an impairment of supply of products.

Except for the two mentioned exceptions, price control measures are not the proper means for the authority to direct the market economy into the desired channels. The forces of the market prove stronger than the power of the authority. The authority has to face the alternatives, either to accept the law of the market as it stands, or to attempt to replace the market and the market economy by a system without the market, that is, by socialism.

3. Minimum Wages and Unemployment

Of greatest practical importance among the measures of price-fixing policy are wage scales determined by trade union action. In some countries minimum-wage rates were established by direct government action. The governments of other countries interfere with wages indirectly only, by acquiescing in the application of active pressure by unions and their members against enterprises and those willing to work who do not abide by their wage orders. The authoritatively fixed wage rate tends to cause permanent unemployment of a considerable part of the labor force. Here again the government usually intervenes by granting unemployment relief.

When we speak of wages we shall always mean real wages, not money wages. It is obvious that a change in the purchasing power of the monetary unit must be followed, sooner or later, by a change in the nominal money rate of wages.

Economists were always fully aware that wages, too, were a market phenomenon and that there were forces operative in the market which, should wages depart from market wages, tend to bring wages back to the point conforming to market conditions. If wages fall below the point prescribed by the market, then the competition of entrepreneurs who seek workers will raise them again. If wages rise above the market level, part of the demand for labor will be eliminated and the pressure of those who become unemployed will make wages fall again. Even Karl Marx and the Marxists have always maintained that it is impossible for the trade unions to raise the wages of all workers permanently above the level established by market conditions. The advocates of unionism have never answered this argument. They have merely condemned economics as a "dismal science."

To deny that raising wages above the point prescribed by market conditions must necessarily lead to a reduction in the number of employed workers is tantamount to asserting that the size of the labor supply has no influence on wage rates. A few remarks will prove the fallacy of such assertions. Why are opera tenors so highly paid? Because the supply is very small. If the supply of opera tenors were as large as the supply of chauffeurs, their incomes would, given a corresponding demand, immediately sink to the level of chauffeur wages. What does the entrepreneur do if he requires especially skilled workers of whom only a limited number is available? He raises the wages he offers in order to induce workers to leave competing entrepreneurs and to attract those he seeks.

As long as only one part of the labor force, mostly skilled workers, was unionized, the wage raise forced by the union did not lead to unemployment but caused wages for unskilled labor to fall. The skilled workers who lost their jobs in consequence of the wage policy of the trade unions entered the market for unskilled labor and thereby increased the supply. The corollary of higher wages for organized labor was lower wages for unorganized labor. But, as soon as labor in all lines of production becomes organized, the situation changes. Then, the workers who become unemployed in one industry can no longer find employment in other lines; they remain unemployed.

The trade unions testify to the validity of this point of view when they try to prevent the influx of workers into their industry or into their country. When the trade unions refuse to admit new members or make their admission more difficult by high initiation fees, or when they fight immigration, they prove themselves convinced that a larger number of workers could only be employed if wages were lowered.

Also by recommending credit expansion* as a means of reducing unemployment, the trade unions admit the soundness of the wage theory of the economists whom they otherwise dismiss as "orthodox." Credit expansion reduces the value of the monetary unit and thus makes prices rise. If money wages remain stable or at least do not rise to the same extent as commodity prices, this means a reduction of real wages. Lower real wages make it possible to employ more workers.

Finally, we have to consider it a tribute to the "orthodox" wage theory that the trade unions impose upon themselves restrictions in their fixing of wage rates. The same methods by which trade unions force the entrepreneur to pay wages which are 10 percent above the rates which would prevail in the unhampered market might make it possible to bring about even considerably higher wages. Why, therefore, not ask for a wage increase of 50 percent, or 100 percent? The trade unions refrain from such a policy because they know that an even greater number of their members would lose their jobs.

The economist considers wages a market phenomenon; he is of the opinion that at any given moment wages are determined by the prevailing data of the market supply of material means of production and of labor, and by the demand for consumers' goods. If by an act of intervention wages are fixed at a point higher than the one given by market conditions, a part of the labor supply cannot be employed; unemployment rises. It is precisely the same situation as in the case of

* [See chapter III.—Editor]

commodities. If the owners of commodities ask a price above the market they cannot sell their entire stock.

If, however, as those who advocate wage fixing by unions or by government maintain, wages are not definitely determined by the market, the question arises, why should wages not be made to rise still higher? It is, of course, desirable to have the workers receive as large incomes as possible. What then deters the trade unions, if not the fear of larger unemployment?

To this, the trade unions reply, we are not after high wages; all we want is "fair wages." But what is "fair" in this case? If the raising of wages by intervention does not have effects which are injurious to labor's interests, then it certainly is unfair not to go still further in raising wages. What prevents the trade unions and the government officials, who are entrusted with the arbitration of wage disputes, from raising the wages still more?

In some countries it was demanded that wages be fixed in such a way as to confiscate all the income of entrepreneurs and capitalists, other than salary for managerial activity, and to distribute it to the wage earners. To achieve this, orders were issued prohibiting the dismissal of workers without special permission of the government. By this measure an increase in unemployment was prevented in the short run. But it caused other effects which in the long run were contrary to the interests of the workers. If entrepreneurs and capitalists do not receive profits and interest payments they will not starve or ask for charity; they will live on their capital. The consumption of capital, however, changes the ratio of capital to labor, lowers the marginal productivity of labor, and thus ultimately lowers wages. It is in the interest of the wage earners that capital should not be consumed.

It should be emphasized that the preceding statements refer to one aspect only of trade union activity, namely their policy to raise wages above the rates which would prevail in the unhampered market. What other activities the trade unions are carrying on or might undertake has no bearing on the subject.

4. The Political Consequences of Unemployment

Unemployment as a permanent phenomenon of considerable magnitude has become the foremost political problem of all democratic countries. That millions are permanently excluded from the productive process is a condition which cannot be tolerated for any length of time. The unemployed individual wants work. He wants to earn because he considers the opportunities which wages afford higher than the doubtful value of permanent leisure in poverty. He despairs because he is unable to find work. From among the unemployed, the adventurers and the aspiring dictators select their storm troopers.

Public opinion regards the pressure of unemployment as a proof of the failure of the market economy. The public believes that capitalism has shown its inability to solve the problems of social cooperation. Unemployment appears as the inescapable result of the antinomies, the contradictions, of the capitalistic economy. Public opinion fails to realize that the real cause for the permanent and large unemployment is to be sought in the wage policy of the trade unions and in the assistance granted to such policy by the government. The voice of the economist does not reach the public.

Laymen have always believed that technological progress deprived people of their livelihood. For this reason the guilds persecuted every inventor; for this reason craftsmen destroyed machines. Today the opponents of technological progress have the support of men who are commonly regarded as scientists. In books and articles it is asserted that technological unemployment is unavoidable—in the capitalistic system, at least. As a means to fight unemployment shorter working hours are recommended; as weekly wages are to remain stable or to be lowered less than proportionately, or even increased, this means in most cases further wage rate raises and thus increased unemployment. Public works projects are recommended as a means to provide employment. But if the necessary funds are secured by issuing government bonds or by taxation, the situation remains unchanged. The funds used for the relief projects are withdrawn from other production, the increase of employment opportunities is counteracted by a decrease of employment opportunities in other branches of the economic system.

Finally credit expansion and inflation are resorted to. But with rising prices and falling real wages the trade union demands for higher wages are gaining momentum. However, we have to note that devaluations and similar inflationary measures have, in some instances, been temporarily successful in alleviating the effects of union wage policy and in halting temporarily the growth of unemployment.

Compared with the ineffectual handling of the unemployment problem by countries which customarily are called democratic, the policy of dictatorships appears extremely successful. Unemployment disappears if compulsory labor is introduced by inducting the unemployed into the army and other military units, into labor camps and similar compulsory service. The workers in these services must be satisfied with wages which are far below those of other workers. Gradually an approximation of wage rates is sought by raising the wages of the service workers and by lowering the wages of other workers. The political successes of the totalitarian countries are primarily based on the results which they achieved in the fight against service workers and by lowering the wages of other workers. The political successes of the totalitarian countries are primarily based on the results which they achieved in the fight against unemployment.

III.

Inflation and Credit Expansion

1. Inflation

Inflationism is that policy which by increasing the quantity of money or credit seeks to raise money prices and money wages or seeks to counteract a decline of money prices and money wages which threatens as the result of an increase in the supply of consumers' goods.

In order to understand the economic significance of inflationism we have to refer to a fundamental law of monetary theory. This law says: The service which money renders to the economic community is independent of the amount of money. Whether the absolute amount of money in a closed economic system is large or small does not matter. In the long run the purchasing power of the monetary unit will establish itself at the point at which the demand for money will equal the quantity of money. The fact that each individual would like to have more money should not deceive us. Everybody wants to be richer, to have more goods, and he expresses it by saying he wants more money. But were he to receive additional money, he would spend it by increasing his consumption, or by increasing his investments; he would in the long run neither increase his ready cash at all, nor increase it significantly compared with the increase in his supply of goods and services. Furthermore, the satisfaction which he derives from the receipt of additional money will depend on his receiving a larger share of the additional money than others and on receiving it earlier than others. An inhabitant of Berlin, who in 1914 would have been jubilant upon receiving an unexpected legacy of 1,000 marks, did not think an amount of 1,000,000,000 marks worth his attention in the fall of 1923.

If we disregard the function of money as a standard of deferred payments, that is, the fact that there are obligations and claims expressed in fixed amounts of money maturing in the future, we easily recognize that it does not matter for a closed economy whether its total quantity of money is x million money units or $100x$ million money units. In the latter case prices and wages will simply be expressed in larger quantities of the monetary unit.

What the advocates of inflation desire and the proponents of sound money oppose is not the ultimate result of inflation, namely, the increase of the money quantity itself, but rather the effects of the process by which the additional money enters the economic system and gradually changes prices and wages. The social consequences of inflation are twofold: (1) the meaning of all deferred payments is altered to the advantage of the debtors and to the disadvantage of the creditors, or (2) the price changes do not occur simultaneously nor to the same extent for all individual commodities and services. Therefore, as long as the inflation has not exerted its full effects on prices and wages there are groups in the community which gain, and groups which lose. Those gain who are in a position to sell the goods and services they are offering at higher prices, while they are still paying the old low prices for the goods and services they are buying. On the other hand, those lose who have to pay higher prices, while still receiving lower prices for their own products and services. If, for instance, the government increases the quantity of money in order to pay for armaments, the entrepreneurs and workers of the munitions industries will be the first to realize inflationary gains. Other groups will suffer from the rising prices until the prices for their products and services go up as well. It is on this time lag between the changes in the prices of various commodities and services that the import-discouraging and export-promoting effect* of the lowering of the purchasing power of the domestic money is based.

Because the effects which the inflationists seek by inflation are of a temporary nature only, there can never be enough inflation from the inflationist point of view. Once the quantity of money ceases to increase, the groups who were reaping gains during the inflation lose their privileged position. They may keep the gains they realized during the inflation but they cannot make any further gains. The gradual rise of the prices of goods which they previously were buying at comparatively low prices now impairs their position because as sellers they can-

---

* [By introducing additional domestic money, the purchasing power of each unit is lowered and the relative value of foreign moneys or foreign exchange is raised. Thus imports become more expensive and are discouraged while exports are encouraged because they are less expensive.—Editor]

not expect prices to rise further. The clamor for inflation will therefore persist.

But on the other hand inflation cannot continue indefinitely. As soon as the public realizes that the government does not intend to stop inflation, that the quantity of money will continue to increase with no end in sight, and that consequently the money prices of all goods and services will continue to soar with no possibility of stopping them, everybody will tend to buy as much as possible and to keep his ready cash at a minimum. The keeping of cash under such conditions involves not only the costs usually called interest, but also considerable losses due to the decrease in the money's purchasing power. The advantages of holding cash must be bought at sacrifices which appear so high that everybody restricts more and more his ready cash. During the great inflations of World War I, this development was termed "a flight to commodities" and the "crack-up boom." The monetary system is then bound to collapse; a panic ensues; it ends in a complete devaluation of money. Barter is substituted or a new kind of money is resorted to. Examples are the Continental currency in 1781, the French assignats in 1796, and the German mark in 1923.

Many false arguments are used to defend inflationism. Least harmful is the claim that a moderate inflation does not do much harm. This has to be admitted. A small dose of poison is less pernicious than a large one. But this is no justification for administering the poison in the first place.

It is claimed that in times of a grave emergency the use of means may be justified which in normal times would not be considered. But who is to decide whether the emergency is grave enough to warrant the application of dangerous measures? Every government and every political party in power is inclined to regard the difficulties it has to cope with as quite extraordinary and to conclude that any means for combating them is justified. The drug addict, who says he will abstain from tomorrow on, will never conquer the drug habit. We have to adopt a sound policy today, not tomorrow.

It is frequently asserted that an inflation is impossible as long as there are unemployed workers and idle machines. This, too, is a dangerous error. If, in the course of an inflation, money wages first remain unchanged and consequently real wages fall, more workers can be employed as long as this condition prevails. But this does not alter the other effects of inflation. Whether idle plants will resume operations depends on whether the prices of the goods they are able to produce will be among those first affected by the price rise due to inflation. If this is not the case the inflation will fail to put them back to work.

Even worse is the error underlying the assertion that we cannot speak of inflation when the increased quantity of money corresponds to a rising output of the means of production and productive facilities. It is irrelevant as far as changes in prices and wages due to the inflation are concerned for what purposes the additional money is being spent. No matter how the means for spending are procured, the interests of a community and its citizens are better served under all conditions by building streets, houses, and plants than by destroying streets, houses, and plants. But this has nothing to do with the problem of inflation. Its effects on prices and production make themselves felt even if it is used to finance useful projects.

Inflation, the issue of additional paper money, and credit expansion are always intentional; they are never acts of God which strike people, like an earthquake. No matter how great and how urgent a need may be, it can only be satisfied from available goods, by goods which are produced by restricting other consumption. The inflation does not produce additional goods, it determines only how much each individual citizen is to sacrifice. Like taxes or government borrowing, it is a means of financing, not a means of satisfying demand.

It is maintained that inflation is unavoidable in times of war. This, too, is an error. An increase in the quantity of money does not create war materials—either directly or indirectly. Rather we should say, if a government does not dare to disclose to the people the bill for the war expenditures and does not dare impose the restrictions on consumption which cannot be avoided, it will prefer inflation to the other two means of financing, namely taxation and borrowing. In any case, increased armaments and war must be paid for by people through restriction of other consumption. But it is politically expedient—even though fundamentally undemocratic—to tell the people that increased armaments and war create boom conditions and increase wealth. In any event, inflation is a shortsighted policy.

Many groups welcome inflation because it harms the creditor and benefits the debtor. It is thought to be a measure for the poor and against the rich. It is surprising to what extent traditional concepts persist even under completely changed conditions. At one time, the rich were creditors, the poor for the most part were debtors. But in the time of bonds, debentures, savings banks, insurance, and social security, things are different. The rich have invested their wealth in plants, warehouses, houses, estates, and common stock and consequently are debtors more often than creditors. On the other hand, the poor—except for farmers—are more often creditors than debtors. By pursuing a policy against the creditor one injures the savings of the masses. One injures particularly the middle classes, the professional man, the endowed foundations, and the universities. Every beneficiary of social security also falls victim to an anti-creditor policy.

It is not necessary specifically to discuss the counterpart of inflationism, namely deflationism. Deflation is unpopular for the very reason that it furthers the interests of the creditors at the expense of the debtors. No political party and no government has ever tried to make a conscious deflationary effort. The unpopularity of deflation is evidenced by the fact that inflationists constantly talk of the evils of deflation in order to give their demands for inflation and credit expansion the appearances of justification.

2. Credit Expansion

It is a fundamental fact of human behavior that people value present goods higher than future goods. An apple available for immediate consumption is valued higher than an apple which will be available next year. And an apple which will be available in a year is in turn valued higher than an apple which will become available in five years. This difference in valuation appears in the market economy in the form of the discount, to which future goods are subject as compared to present goods. In money transactions this discount is called interest.

Interest therefore cannot be abolished. In order to do away with interest we would have to prevent people from valuing a house, which today is habitable, more highly than a house which will not be ready for use for ten years. Interest is not peculiar to the capitalistic system only. In a socialist community too the fact will have to be considered that a loaf of bread which will not be ready for consumption for another year does not satisfy present hunger.

Interest does not have its origin in the meeting of supply and demand of money loans in the capital market. It is rather the function of the loan market, which in business terms is called the money market (for short-term credit) and the capital market (for long-term credit),

to adjust the interest rates for loans transacted in money to the difference in the valuation of present and future goods. This difference in
valuation is the real source of interest. An increase in the quantity of
money, no matter how large, cannot in the long run influence the rate
of interest.

No other economic law is less popular than this, that interest rates
are, in the long run, independent of the quantity of money. Public
opinion is reluctant to recognize interest as a market phenomenon.
Interest is thought to be an evil, an obstacle to human welfare, and,
therefore, it is demanded that it be eliminated or at least considerably
reduced. And credit expansion is considered the proper means to bring
about "easy money."

There is no doubt that credit expansion leads to a reduction of the
interest rate in the short run. At the beginning, the additional supply
of credit forces the interest rate for money loans below the point which
it would have in an unmanipulated market. But it is equally clear that
even the greatest expansion of credit cannot change the difference in
the valuation of future and present goods. The interest rate must ultimately return to the point at which it corresponds to this difference in
the valuation of goods. The description of this process of adjustment
is the task of that part of economics which is called the theory of the
business cycle.

At every constellation of prices, wages, and interest rates, there are
projects which will not be carried out because a calculation of their
profitability shows that there is no chance for the success of such un-
dertakings. The businessman does not have the courage to start the
enterprise because his calculations convince him that he will not gain,
but will lose by it.

This unattractiveness of the project is not a consequence of money
or credit conditions; it is due to the scarcity of economic goods and
labor and to the fact that they have to be devoted to more urgent and
therefore more attractive uses.

When the interest rate is artificially lowered by credit expansion the
false impression is created that enterprises which previously had been
regarded as unprofitable now become profitable. Easy money induces
the entrepreneurs to embark upon businesses which they would not
have undertaken at a higher interest rate. With the money borrowed
from the banks they enter the market with additional demand and
cause a rise in wages and in the prices of the means of production.

This boom of course would have to collapse immediately in the absence of further credit expansion, because these price increases would make the new enterprises appear unprofitable again. But if the banks continue with the credit expansion this brake fails to work. The boom continues.

But the boom cannot continue indefinitely. There are two alternatives. Either the banks continue the credit expansion without restriction and thus cause constantly mounting price increases and an ever-growing orgy of speculation, which, as in all other cases of unlimited inflation, ends in a "crack-up boom" and in a collapse of the money and credit system.[1] Or the banks stop before this point is reached, voluntarily renounce further credit expansion, and thus bring about the crisis. The depression follows in both instances.

It is obvious that a mere banking process like credit expansion cannot create more goods and wealth. What the credit expansion actually accomplishes is to introduce a source of error in the calculations of the entrepreneurs and thus causes them to misjudge business and investment projects. The entrepreneurs act as if more producers' goods were available than are actually at hand. They plan expansion of production on a scale for which the available quantities of producers' goods are not sufficient. These plans are bound to fail because of the deficiency in the available amount of producers' goods. The result is that there are plants which cannot be used because the complementary facilities are lacking; there are plants which cannot be completed; there are other plants again whose products cannot be sold because consumers desire other products more urgently which cannot be produced in sufficient quantities because the necessary productive facilities are not ready. The boom is not *over*-investment, it is *misdirected* investment.

It is frequently argued against this conclusion that it would hold true only if at the beginning of the credit expansion there were neither unused capacity nor unemployment. If there were unemployment and idle capacity, things would be different, they claim. But these assumptions do not affect the argument.

The fact that a part of the productive capacity which cannot be diverted to other uses is unused is the consequence of errors of the past. Investments were made in the past under assumptions which proved to be incorrect; the market now demands something else than what

---

1. As explained in this section on "Credit Expansion."

can be produced by these facilities.[2] The accumulation of inventories is speculation. The owner does not want to sell the goods at the current market price because he hopes to realize a higher price at a future date. Unemployment of workers is also an aspect of speculation. The worker does not want to change his location or occupation, nor does he want to lower his wage demands because he hopes to find the work he prefers at the place he prefers and at higher wages. Both the owners of merchandise and the unemployed refuse to adjust themselves to market conditions because they hope for new data which would change market conditions to their advantage. Because they do not make the necessary adjustments the economic system cannot reach "equilibrium."

In the opinion of the advocates of credit expansion, what is necessary fully to utilize the unused capacity, to sell the supply at prices acceptable to the owners, and to enable the unemployed to find work at wages satisfactory to them is merely additional credit which such expansion could provide. This is the view which underlies all plans for "pump priming." It would be correct for the stocks of goods and for the unemployed under two conditions: (1) if the price rises caused by the additional quantity of money and credit would uniformly and simultaneously affect all other prices and wages, and (2) if the owners of the excessive supplies and the unemployed would not increase their prices and wage demands. This would cause the exchange ratios between these goods and services and other goods and services to change in the same way as they would have to be changed in the absence of credit expansion, by reducing the price and wage demands in order to find buyers and employers.

The course of the boom is not any different because, at its inception, there are unused productive capacity, unsold stocks of goods, and unemployed workers. We might assume, for instance, that we are dealing with copper mines, copper inventories, and copper miners. The price of copper is at a point at which a number of mines cannot profitably continue their production; their workers must remain idle if they do not want to change jobs; and the owners of the copper stocks can only sell part of it if they are unwilling to accept a lower price. What is needed to put the idle mines and miners back to work and to dispose of the copper supply without a price drop is an increase (p) in producers'

---

2. In the absence of credit expansion there also may be plants which are not fully utilized. But they do not disturb the market any more than does the unused submarginal land.

goods in general, which would permit an expansion of overall production, so that an increase in the price, sales, and production of copper would follow. If this increase (p) does not occur, but the entrepreneurs are induced by credit expansion to act as if it had occurred, the effects on the copper market will first be the same as if p actually had appeared. But everything that has been said before of the effects of credit expansion develops in this case as well. The sole difference is that misdirected capital investment, as far as copper is concerned, does not necessitate the withdrawal of capital and labor from other branches of production, which under existing conditions are considered more important by the consumers. But this is only due to the fact that, as far as copper is concerned, the credit expansion boom impinges upon previously misdirected capital and labor which have not yet been adjusted by the normal corrective processes of the price mechanism.

The true meaning of the argument of unused capacity, unsold—or, as it is said inaccurately, unsalable—inventories, and idle labor now becomes apparent. The beginning of every credit expansion encounters such remnants of older, misdirected capital investments and apparently "corrects" them. In actuality, it does nothing but disturb the workings of the adjustment process. The existence of unused means of production does not invalidate the conclusions of the monetary theory of the business cycle. The advocates of credit expansion are mistaken when they believe that, in view of unused means of production, the suppression of all possibilities of credit expansion would perpetuate the depression. The measures they propose would not perpetuate real prosperity, but would constantly interfere with the process of readjustment and the return of normal conditions.

It is impossible to explain the cyclical changes of business on any basis other than the theory which commonly is referred to as the monetary theory of the business cycle. Even those economists who refuse to recognize in the monetary theory the proper explanation of the business cycle have never attempted to deny the validity of its conclusions about the effects of credit expansion. In order to defend their theories about the business cycle, which differ from the monetary theory, they still have to admit that the upswing cannot occur without simultaneous credit expansion, and that the end of the credit expansion also marks the turning point of the cycle. The opponents of the monetary theory actually confine themselves to the assertion that the upswing of the cycle is not caused by credit expansion, but by other factors, and that the credit expansion, without which the upswing would be impossible, is not the result of a policy intended to lower the interest rate and to invite the execution of additional business plans, but that it is released somehow by conditions leading to the upswing without intervention by the banks or by the authorities.

It has been asserted that the credit expansion is released by the rise in the rate of interest through the failure of the banks to raise their interest rates in accordance with the rise in the "natural" rate.[3] This argument too misses the main point of the monetary theory of the cycle. Whether the credit expansion gets under way because the banks ease credit terms, or because they fail to stiffen the terms in accordance with changed market conditions, is of minor importance. Decisive only is the fact that there is credit expansion because there exist institutions which consider it their task to influence interest rates by the granting of additional credit.[4] Whoever believes that credit expansion is a necessary factor in the movement which forces the economy into the upswing, which must be followed by a crisis and depression, would have to admit that the surest means to achieve a cycle-proof economic system lies in preventing credit expansion. But despite the general agreement that measures should be taken to smooth the wave-like movements of the cycle, measures to prevent credit expansion do not receive consideration. Business cycle policy is given the task to perpetuate the upswing created by the credit expansion and yet to prevent the break-down. Proposals to prevent credit expansion are refuted because supposedly they would perpetuate the depression. Nothing could be a more convincing proof of the theory which explains the business cycle as originating from interventions in favor of easy money than the obstinate refusal to abandon credit expansion.

One would have to ignore all facts of recent economic history were one to deny that measures to lower rates are considered desirable and that credit expansion is regarded as the most reliable means to achieve this aim. The fact that the smooth functioning and the development

3. [Fritz] Machlup (*The Stock Market, Credit and Capital Formation*, London, 1940, p. 248) speaks of "passive inflationism."
4. If a bank is unable to expand credit it cannot create an upswing even if it lowers its interest rate below the market rate. It would merely make a gift to its debtors. The conclusion to be drawn from the monetary theory of the cycle with regard to stabilizing measures is not the postulate that the banks should not lower the interest rate, but that they should not expand credit. This [Gottfried] Haberler (*Prosperity and Depression*, League of Nations, Geneva, 1939, p. 65ff.) misunderstood and therefore his criticisms are untenable.

and steady progress of the economy is over and over again disturbed by artificial booms and ensuing depressions is not a necessary characteristic of the market economy. It is rather the inevitable consequence of repeated interventions which intend to create easy money by credit expansion.

3. Foreign Exchange Control

An attempt by government forcibly to give the national credit money or paper money a value higher than its market price causes effects which Gresham's Law describes. A condition results which generally is called a shortage of foreign exchange. This expression is misleading. Anyone who offers less than the market price for any good is unable to buy it; this holds true for foreign exchange just as much as for all other goods.

It is an essential characteristic of an economic good that it is not so abundant that it can satisfy all desired uses. A good of which in this sense there would not be a shortage would be a free good. As money is necessarily an economic good, not a free good, money of which there would not be a shortage is inconceivable. The governments, which adopt an inflationary policy but at the same time pretend that they have not lowered the purchasing power of the domestic money, have something else in mind when they complain about a shortage of foreign exchange. Were the government to refrain from any further action once it had increased the quantity of the domestic money by inflation, the value of the domestic money would fall relative to metallic money and foreign exchange and its purchasing power would decline. However, there would not be a "shortage" of metallic money and foreign exchange. Those who were ready to pay the market price would obtain for their domestic money any desired amount of metallic money or foreign exchange. Those who buy goods have to pay the market price given by the exchange rate of the market; they either have to pay in metallic money (or foreign exchange) or pay that amount of domestic money which is determined by the market rate for foreign exchange.

But the government is unwilling to accept these consequences. Being sovereign it believes itself omnipotent. It can issue penal laws; it has courts and police, gallows and jails at its disposal and can destroy anyone who rebels. Consequently, it orders that prices are not to rise. On the one hand, the government prints additional money, enters the market with it, and thus creates an additional demand for goods. On the other hand it orders that prices should not rise, because government thinks it can do anything at will.

We have already dealt with the attempts to fix the prices of goods and services. Now we have to consider the attempts to fix the rates of foreign exchange.

The government places the blame for the rise of foreign exchange rates on the unfavorable balance of payments and on speculation. Being unwilling to abandon the price fixing for foreign exchange, it takes measures to reduce the demand. Foreign exchange is to be bought only by those who require it for a purpose of which the government approves. Goods, the importation of which the government considers superfluous, should not be imported any longer; interest and amortization payments to foreign creditors are to be discontinued; citizens are not to travel abroad. The government fails to realize that its efforts to "improve" the balance of payments are futile. If less is imported, less can be exported. Citizens who spend less on trips abroad, imported goods, and interest and repayment of foreign loans will not use the unspent money to increase their ready cash; they will spend it within the country and thus raise prices in the domestic market. Because prices rise, because citizens buy more within the country, less will be exported. Prices rise not only because imports have become more expensive in terms of domestic money; they rise because the quantity of money was increased and because the citizens display a greater demand for domestic goods.

The government believes that it can accomplish its purpose by nationalizing dealing in foreign exchange. Those who receive foreign exchange—from export transactions, for instance—must by law deliver it to the government and receive in exchange only the amount of domestic money which corresponds to the foreign exchange price which has been fixed by the government below the market price. Were this principle to be enforced consistently, exports would cease entirely. As the government does not want this effect it finally has to give in. It grants subsidies to the export trade intended to compensate for losses which the exporters suffer by the obligation to turn over to the government at the fixed price the foreign exchange they receive.

On the other hand the government sells foreign exchange to those who want to use it for purposes which meet with the approval of the government. Were the government to adhere to its fiction and to demand only the official price for this foreign exchange this would amount to subsidizing the importers (not the import trade). As this is not intended by the government, compensation is sought, for instance, by a proportionate raising of import duties or by imposing special taxes on the profits and transactions of the importers.

Control of foreign exchange means the nationalization of foreign trade and of all business with foreign countries. It does not alter foreign exchange rates. Whether or not the government suppresses the publication of actual foreign exchange rates which reflect market conditions is immaterial. In foreign trade transactions only those rates are significant which reflect the purchasing power of domestic money.

The effects of such a nationalization of all economic relations with foreign countries on the life of the individual citizen are the more decisive the smaller the country and the more closely connected are its international economic relations. Foreign travel, attendance at foreign universities, and the reading of books and newspapers published abroad are only possible if the government places the necessary foreign exchange at the individual's disposal. As a means of lowering the price of foreign exchange, the control is a complete failure. But it is an effective implement of dictatorship.

4. The Flight of Capital and the Problem of "Hot Money"

It is claimed that foreign exchange control is necessary to prevent the flight of capital.

If a capitalist fears complete or partial confiscation of his property by the government, he seeks to save whatever he can. It is, however, impossible to withdraw capital from enterprises and to transfer it to another country without heavy losses. If there is a general fear of confiscation by the government, the price paid for going businesses drops to the level which reflects the probability of such confiscation. In October 1917, enterprises in Russia which represented investments of millions of gold rubles were offered for the equivalent of a few pennies; later on they became completely unsalable.

The term "capital flight" is misleading. The capital invested in enterprises, buildings, and estates cannot flee; it can only change hands. The state which intends to confiscate does not lose anything by it. The new owner becomes the victim of the confiscation instead of the previous owner.

Only the entrepreneur who has recognized the danger of confiscation in time is able to avoid the threatening loss by means other than the sale of his entire business. He may refrain from renewing the parts of the equipment which become used up and worn out, and he may transfer the amounts he thus saves to other countries. He may leave abroad funds resulting from export transactions. If he uses the first means his plant will sooner or later cease to be productive or, at least, competitive. If he chooses the latter he will have to restrict or even close down his production because of the lack of working capital, unless he can borrow additional funds.

With this exception a state which intends to confiscate, completely or partially, the enterprises located in its territory does not run the risk of losing part of its spoils by the flight of capital.

The owners of money, promissory notes, deposits, and other claims find themselves in a better position than the owners of enterprises and real property. They, however, are threatened not only by confiscation; inflation too may deprive them of all or part of their property. But they are the ones who are able to buy foreign exchange and to transfer their capital abroad because their property consists of ready cash.

The governments do not like to admit this. They believe it to be the duty of every citizen to suffer quietly the confiscatory measures; and this even in the case when—as in inflation—the measures do not benefit the state but only certain individual citizens. One of the tasks assigned to foreign exchange control is to prevent such a flight of capital.

Let us look at an historic example. During the first years following the armistice of 1918, it was possible to sell abroad German, Austrian, and Hungarian bank notes, bonds, and debentures payable in the currencies of these countries. The governments impeded such sales either directly or indirectly by forcing their subjects to give up the foreign exchange received in such transactions. Did the German, Austrian, or Hungarian economies become richer or poorer by this intervention? Let us assume that in 1920 Austrians succeeded in selling Austrian mortgage bonds to foreigners at a price of $10 for each 1,000 *kronen* par value. The Austrian creditor would thus have salvaged about 5 percent of the nominal value of his claim. The Austrian debtor would not have been affected at all. However, when the Austrian debtor had to repay the debt in the nominal value of 1,000 *kronen*, which in 1914 was about $200, the 1,000 *kronen* he repaid in 1922 would have equaled only about 1.4¢. The loss of approximately $9.98 would have been suffered by the foreign holder, not by an Austrian. Could one say, therefore, that a policy which prevented such transactions was justified from the standpoint of Austrian interests?

The holders of ready cash try as far as possible to avoid the dangers of devaluation which today threaten in every country. They keep large bank balances in those countries in which there is the least probability of devaluation in the immediate future. If conditions change and they fear for these funds, they transfer such balances to other countries which for the moment seem to offer greater security. These balances which are always ready to flee—so-called "hot money"—have fundamentally influenced the data and the workings of the international money market. They present a serious problem in the operation of the modern banking system.

During the last hundred years all countries have adopted the single-reserve system. In order to make it easier for the central bank to pursue a policy of domestic credit expansion the other banks were induced to deposit the greater part of their reserves with the central bank. The banks then reduced their vault cash to the amount necessary for the conduct of everyday normal business. They no longer considered it necessary to coordinate their payables and receivables as to maturity so that they should be able to fulfill their obligations at all times fully and promptly. To be able to meet the daily maturing claims of their depositors, they deemed it sufficient to own assets which the central bank considered a satisfactory basis for the granting of credit.

When the influx of "hot money" began the banks did not see any danger in the increase of demand on short-term deposits. Relying on the central bank they accepted the deposits and used them as a basis for extending loans. They were unaware of the danger they were inviting. They did not give any thought to the means which they would someday need to repay those deposits which obviously were always ready to move.

It is argued that the existence of such "hot money" necessitates foreign exchange control. Let us consider the situation in the United States. If, as of June 5, 1933, the United States had not forbidden the private holding of gold, the banks would have been able to carry on a gold deposit business as a particular branch of activity, separate from their other transactions. They would have bought gold for this branch of their activity and would have either held it themselves or deposited it earmarked for safekeeping with the Federal Reserve banks. Thus, this gold would have become sterilized from the standpoint of the American currency and banking system. It is only because the government has intervened by forbidding individuals to own gold that a "hot money" problem comes into being. The fact that the unwelcome effect of one intervention makes other interventions necessary does not justify interventionism.

Of course, the entire problem is today no longer of importance. The fleeing funds have reached their last haven, America. There is no safe place left to which they could escape should this refuge prove vain.

IV

Confiscation and Subsidies

1. Confiscation

The complete confiscation of all private property is tantamount to the introduction of socialism. Therefore we do not have to deal with it in an analysis of the problems of interventionism. We are concerned here only with the partial confiscation of property. Such confiscation is today attempted primarily by taxation.

The ideological motivations of such action is immaterial. The only question of interest to us is merely: What is sought by these measures and what is actually accomplished?

Let us first consider taxes which directly or indirectly affect incomes only. In all countries there is today a tendency to tax larger incomes at higher rates than smaller incomes. In the case of incomes which exceed a certain amount most countries tax away, even nominally, up to 90 percent. Methods prescribed by law for the determination of the amount of income, and the interpretation of these laws by the administering agencies, fix incomes considerably higher than could be established on the basis of sound accounting principles. If taxpayers could not avoid some taxes by using loopholes in the laws, their actual taxes would thus not infrequently exceed by far the amount of their actual incomes. But legislators try to plug these loopholes.

Popular opinion is inclined to believe that the taxing away of huge incomes does not concern the less wealthy classes. This is a fallacy. The recipients of higher incomes usually consume a smaller proportion of their incomes and save and invest a larger part than the less wealthy. And it is only through saving that capital is created. Only that part of income that is not consumed can be accumulated as capital. By making the higher incomes pay a larger share of the public expenditures than lower incomes, one impedes the operation of capital and eliminates the tendency, which prevails in a society with increasing capital, to increase the marginal productivity of labor and therefore to raise wages.

The same is, of course, true even to a greater extent of all methods of taxing away part of the principal. By drawing on capital to pay for public expenditures through inheritance taxes or a capital levy, for instance, capital is directly consumed.

The demagogue tells the voters: "The state has to make large expenditures. But the procurement of funds for these expenditures is not your concern. The rich should be made to pay." The honest politician should say: "*Unfortunately* the state will need more money to cover its expenditures. In any case, you will have to carry most of the burden because you are receiving and consuming the largest share of the total national income. You have to choose between two methods. Either you restrict your consumption immediately, or you consume the capital of the wealthy first and then a bit later you will suffer from falling wages."

The worst type of demagogue goes even further by saying: "We have to arm and possibly even go to war. But this not only will not lower your standard of living; it will even increase it. Right now we shall undertake a large-scale housing program and increase real wages." To this we have to say that with a limited quantity of materials and labor we cannot simultaneously make both armaments and dwellings. Herr Göring* was more honest in this respect. He told his people "guns *or* butter," but not "guns *and* (therefore) still more butter." This honesty is the only thing Herr Göring will be able to claim to his credit before the tribunal of history.

A tax system which would serve the real interests of the wage earners would tax only that part of income which is being consumed, and not saved and invested. High taxes on the *spending* of the rich do not injure the interests of the masses; however, every measure which impedes the formation of capital or which consumes capital does injure them.

Of course, there are circumstances which make the consumption of capital unavoidable. A costly war cannot be financed without such

---

* [Hermann Göring (1893–1946) founded and, until 1936, headed the Gestapo, Nazi Germany's secret police. He was responsible for Germany's pre–World War II rearmament and later became chief of the German air force. In 1946, he was tried by the Allies at Nuremberg, convicted of war crimes, and sentenced to death by hanging. But two hours before his scheduled execution he cheated the gallows by swallowing poison he had cleverly concealed from his captors.—Editor]

a damaging measure. But those who are aware of the effects of capital consumption will try to keep this consumption within the limits of necessity, because that is in the interest of *labor*, not because it is in the interest of *capital*. There may arise situations in which it may be unavoidable to burn down the house to keep from freezing, but those who do that should realize what it costs and what they will have to do without later on. We must emphasize this, particularly at the present moment, in order to refute the current errors about the nature of the armament and war booms.

The costs of extraordinary armaments may be paid for by inflation, by borrowing, or by taxes which hamper the formation of, or which even consume, capital. How inflation leads to boom conditions does not require further explanation. When funds are made available by borrowing, this can only shift investment and production from one field to another; the increase in production and consumption in one sector of the economy is compensated for by the decline of production and consumption in another part. The funds which are withheld from capital formation and withdrawn from already accumulated capital may have the effect of an increase in current consumption. Thus consumption for military purposes may be increased without a proportionate decrease in other consumption. This may be called a "stimulus" to business. But we should not overlook the fact that all the effects of this boom, which are favorably looked upon now, will be paid for by depression and reduced consumption in the future.

2. The Procurement of Funds for Public Expenditure

Hunger can only be satisfied with bread which is already available; future bread does not satisfy anyone today. It would seem superfluous to reiterate such self-evident statements were it not necessary to refute fallacies with regard to the procurement of funds for public expenditure.

War, it is frequently said, is fought not only in our interest, but also in the interest of our children and grandchildren. It is only just that they should bear part of the war costs. Therefore, only part of the war expenditures should be paid out of taxes; the rest should be paid out of borrowing; the interest payments and the amortization of the loans should be the problem of future generations.

This is plain nonsense. A war can be fought only with weapons which are today already available. Material and labor which are placed in the service of armaments, therefore, are withdrawn from our presently available means and diminish the supply of other goods for people living in the present. They are taken out of present income and present property. The grandchildren are concerned only insofar as they will inherit less. This fact cannot be altered by any method of financing.

Even if part of the war expenditures is covered by borrowing, that means resources which otherwise would be devoted to the production of other goods are now used for war purposes. It is only for the man who happens to be secretary of the treasury today that borrowing means a postponement of the payment. For the citizens, borrowing means they pay the bill immediately by forgoing consumption in the present. What one man borrows is, for the duration of the loan, not available to the lender.

An individual may buy a refrigerator on the installment plan if someone grants him the necessary credit. The totality of the citizens of the world or of a closed economy cannot buy anything on credit. Neither can those who are not yet born make loans to us. In this connection, we may disregard foreign loans; they are out of the question for the United States today [1940].

Equally erroneous is the opinion that government borrowing is a measure in favor of the rich. Were we to tax the rich even more than we do now we would have to take away their businesses, that is, we would have to adopt socialism. Because we do not want to go that far and because we do not want to impose higher taxes on the masses, we choose the seemingly painless way of borrowing.

"This," says the socialist, "is precisely the point. You do not want to adopt socialism. Germany, however, proves that socialism is superior in the production of armaments. The German army is the best equipped in the world. The crux of the world problem today is that the Nazis have superior equipment."

This argument, too, misses the point. Germany is well equipped because for at least eight years it has restricted the consumption of the whole population and has placed her entire productive system in the service of armaments. With unbelievable shortsightedness, England, France, and the small democracies failed to arm themselves for defense. Even after the war started they did not take it seriously. The fight against war profiteering seemed to them more important than the fight against the Nazis.

For the armaments industry the same principle holds true as for all other production: Private enterprise is more efficient than public enterprise. A hundred years ago guns and rifles were mostly produced in government arsenals and by small craftsmen. Private entrepreneurs found the production of arms unattractive. It was not until they realized that the nations were only interested in exterminating each other that they took up armament production. Their success was overwhelming. The arms produced by large-scale private industry stood up far better in actual combat [in wars] than the products of state-owned arsenals. All the improvement and perfection of the implements of war have originated in private enterprise. The state-owned arsenals were always backward in accepting new techniques, and the military experts have always been reluctant in accepting the improvements which the entrepreneurs furnished.

Contrary to popular belief, nations do not fight wars in order to make it possible for the arms factories to make money. Arms factories exist because nations fight wars. The entrepreneurs and capitalists who produce arms would manufacture other goods if the demand for arms was not stronger than it is for other goods. Germany's war industry, too, developed as a private enterprise. As a nationalized industry it may be able to maintain for a certain time the advantage it has gained as a private industry.

In England today it is frequently said: If England's workers make the heavy sacrifices which the war imposes on them they have a right to demand that their noble attitude should be rewarded by the abolition of capitalism and the adoption of socialism after the war. There is hardly anything more confused than this argument.

If the workers of England defend their country, their freedom, and their culture against the onslaught of the Nazis and Fascists, and against the Communists, who for all practical purposes are the allies of the Nazis,* they are doing it for themselves and for their children, not for the interests of some other people from whom later on they may demand rewards. The only reward which the great sacrifices may bring them is victory and with it the safeguard that they will not get into the same position in which the German and Russian masses find

---

* [Recall that when Mises wrote these lines, Germany and the Soviets were allies under their 1939 nonaggression treaty until June 22, 1941, when Germany violated that treaty and attacked Soviet Russia.—Editor]

themselves. If the English workers were of the opinion that this prospective success did not warrant taking the burden upon themselves which the war imposes, they would not fight; they would capitulate.

If we believe that socialism is a better system and secures a better existence for the great majority of the population than does capitalism, then we should adopt socialism regardless of war or peace, and irrespective of whether the workers have been brave in the war or not. If we believe, however, that the economic system, which Messrs. Hitler, Stalin, and Mussolini call "plutocracy," guarantees a better life for the masses than socialism, it will not occur to us to "reward" the workers by lowering their standard of living to the level of the Germans, Italians, and Russians.

3. Unprofitable Public Works and Subsidies

The entrepreneurs try to undertake only such projects as appear to promise profits. This means that they endeavor to use the scarce means of production in such a way that the most urgent needs will be satisfied first, and that no part of capital and labor will be devoted to the satisfaction of less urgent needs as long as a more urgent need, for whose satisfaction they could be used, goes unsatisfied.

When the government intervenes to make possible a project which promises not profits, but losses, then there is only talk in public of the need which finds satisfaction through this intervention; we do not hear anything of the needs which fail to be satisfied because the government has diverted to other purposes the means of satisfying them. Only what is gained by the government action is considered, not also what it costs.

The economist is not called upon to tell the people what they should do and how they should use their resources. But it is his duty to call public attention to the costs. This differentiates him from the quack who always speaks only of what the intervention gives, never of what it takes.

Let us, for instance, consider a case which we may judge with objectivity today because it is a matter of the past, though not of a very distant past. It is proposed that a railroad, the construction and operation of which does not promise profitability, is to be made possible by a government subsidy. It may be, it is said, that the railroad is not profitable in the usual sense of the word and that, therefore, it is not attractive to entrepreneurs and capitalists, but it would contribute to the development of the whole region. It would promote trade, commerce, and agriculture and thus it would make an important contribution to the progress of the economy. All this would have to be taken into consideration if the value of this construction and operation is to be judged from a higher standpoint than that of profitability alone. From the standpoint of private interests the construction of the railroad may appear inadvisable. But from the standpoint of the national welfare it seems beneficial.

This reasoning is thoroughly mistaken. Of course, it cannot be denied that the inhabitants of the region through which the railroad is to run would be benefited. Or, more accurately, it gives advantages to the landowners of this region and to those who have made investments there which cannot be transferred elsewhere without a diminution of their value. It is said that it develops the productive forces of the regions through which it runs. The economist has to express this differently: The state pays the subsidies out of the taxpayers' money for the construction, maintenance, and operation of the line which, without this assistance, could not be built and operated. These subsidies shift a part of the production from locations which offer more favorable natural conditions of production to locations which are less suited for this purpose. Land will be cultivated which, in view of its distance from the centers of consumption and in view of its low fertility, could not permit profitable cultivation unless it is subsidized indirectly by financial grants to the transport system, to the cost of which it cannot contribute proportionately. Certainly, these subsidies contribute to the economic development of a region where otherwise less would be produced. But the production increase in the part of the country thus favored by the government's railroad policy is to be contrasted with the burden placed on production and consumption in those parts of the country which have to pay the costs of the government policy. The poorer, less fertile, and more remote land is being subsidized out of the proceeds of taxes, which either burden the production of better land or have to be borne by the consumers directly. The enterprises which are located in the less advantageous region will be able to expand production, but the enterprises in more advantageous locations will have to restrict their production. One may consider this as "just" or politically expedient, but one should not be deluded into believing that it increases the total satisfaction; it reduces it.

One should not consider the increase of production in the region served by the subsidized railroad an "advantage from the standpoint of national welfare." These advantages amount only to this, that a number of enterprises are operating in locations which under different conditions would have been regarded as unfavorable. The privileges which the state grants to these enterprises indirectly by subsidizing the railroads are in no way different from those privileges which the state grants to other less efficient enterprises under different conditions. In the final analysis, the effect is the same whether the state subsidizes or grants privileges to a cobbler's business, for instance, in order to enable him to compete with the shoe manufacturers, or whether it favors land, which due to its location is not competitive, by paying out of public funds part of the costs of transporting its products.

It does not matter whether the state undertakes the unprofitable enterprise itself, or whether it subsidizes a private business so that it may undertake the unprofitable enterprise. The effect on the community is identical in both instances. The method used in granting the subsidy is not important either. It does not matter whether the less efficient producer is subsidized so that he may produce or increase his production, or whether the more efficient producer is subsidized so that he will not produce, or will restrict his production. It is immaterial whether bounties are paid for producing or for not producing, or whether the government buys up the products to withhold them from the market. In each case the citizens pay twice—once as taxpayers who indirectly pay the subsidy, and then again as consumers in higher prices for the goods they buy and in reduced consumption.

4. "Altruistic" Entrepreneurship

When the self-styled "progressives" use the word profit they rant and rave. They would like completely to eliminate profits. In their view, the entrepreneur should serve the people altruistically, not seek profits. He is either not to receive anything, or to be content, if his business is successful, with a small margin over his actual costs. That the entrepreneur has to bear the possible loss is never objected to.

But the profit orientation of the activities of entrepreneurs is precisely what gives sense and meaning, guidance and direction, to the market economy based on private ownership of the means of production.

To eliminate the profit motive is to transform the market economy into chaos.

We have already dealt with the confiscation of profits and the effects of such action. Now, we shall discuss the limitation of profits to a definite percentage of costs. If the entrepreneur is to receive more, the higher his costs rise, his incentive to produce as cheaply as possible is changed to the opposite. Every reduction in production costs reduces his receipts; every increase in production costs means more income for him. We do not have to presuppose here a sinister intention on the part of the entrepreneur. We merely have to understand what a cut in production costs involves for the entrepreneur.

For the most part, the entrepreneur can achieve cost reductions in two different ways: By careful purchases of raw materials and semi-finished products, and by adopting more efficient methods of production. Both involve a high degree of risk and the exercise of intelligence and foresight. Like every other action of the entrepreneur, whether the most opportune moment to purchase has come, or whether it is better to wait longer, is speculation on an uncertain future. The entrepreneur who bears the entire loss but participates in only a part of the gain, his share increasing with rising expenditures, is in a different position from the entrepreneur who is credited *or* debited with the entire profit *or* loss. His attitude toward the risks of the market will be fundamentally altered. He will be inclined, therefore, to buy at higher market prices than the entrepreneur in the free economy. The same is true of improvements in production methods. They too are always risky; additional investments are necessary of which it cannot be said with certainty in advance whether they will pay. Why should an entrepreneur take chances if, in case of success, he is to be punished by a reduction in his receipts?

V.

Corporativism and Syndicalism

1. Corporativism

Corporativism[1] is a program, not a reality. This has to be stated at the very beginning to avoid misunderstandings. Nowhere was it attempted to translate this program into actuality. Even in Italy, in spite of the constant propaganda talk, nothing has really been done to establish the system of the corporative state (*stato corporativo*).

It has been attempted to characterize the different political and economic ideologies as peculiar to certain nations. Western ideas have been contrasted with the German and Slavic ideas; a difference was supposedly discovered between the Latin and the Teutonic mentality; particularly in Russia and Germany there is talk of the mission of the chosen people which is destined to rule the world and to bring it salvation. In view of such tendencies it is necessary to emphasize that all political and economic ideas which dominate the world today have been developed by English, Scottish, and French thinkers. Neither the Germans nor the Russians have contributed one iota to the concepts of socialism; the socialist ideas came to Germany and Russia from the West just as did the ideas which many Germans and Russians today stigmatize as Western. The same is true of the program of corporativism. It stems from English guild socialism and it is necessary to study the writings of this today almost-forgotten movement in order to obtain

1. Corporativism—the name given to the particular Italian brand of economic organization (*economia corporativa*; in German, *Staendestaat*) proposed during the Mussolini era. [Corporativism was to grant complete autonomy to every branch of business or "guild," with absolute authority over its own internal affairs, wages, hours, production, and so on. Matters affecting other businesses were to be settled by inter-guild arbitration or government ruling. Such an arrangement is unrealizable and, therefore, was never implemented. For further details, see Mises's *Human Action* (2nd–4th and Liberty Fund eds., pp. 816–820); also alphabetical entry in Percy L. Greaves, Jr.'s glossary in the Liberty Fund edition.—Editor]

information about the basic ideas of corporativism. The Italian, Portuguese, and Austrian publications, party programs, and other commentaries concerning the corporative state lack precision of meaning and avoid exact formulations and statements; they gloss over the real difficulties by making wide use of popular slogans. The English guild socialists, however, show more clarity in the presentation of the program, and Sidney and Beatrice Webb have given a complete statement of the aim and operation of this system.[2]

In the corporativist utopia the market is replaced by the interplay of what the Italians call corporatives, that is, compulsory organizations of all people engaged in a certain industry. Everything that concerns this industry only, that is to say, the internal affairs of the individual corporatives, is handled by the corporative itself without interference from the state or from persons not belonging to the particular corporative.[3] The relations between the different corporatives are regulated by negotiation between them or by a joint conference of representatives of all corporatives. The state, that is the parliamentary body elected by general vote and the government responsible to it, does not intervene at all, or only when the corporatives fail to reach an agreement.

In drawing up their plans the English guild socialists had in mind the pattern of English local government and its relation to the central government. They proposed creating self-government of the individual industries. Just as the counties and cities take care of their own local affairs the individual branches of production would administer their internal affairs within the structure of the whole social organism.

But in a society which is based on division of labor there are no internal problems of individual businesses, enterprises, or industries which would concern only those connected with such businesses, enterprises, or industries and would not also affect the other citizens. Everybody is interested in seeing that each single business, enterprise, and industry be run as efficiently as given conditions permit. Every waste of labor and material in any industry affects each individual citizen. It is impossible to leave the decisions over the choice of production methods and of the kind and quantity of the products solely to those engaged in an industry because such decisions concern everybody, not only the members of the vocation, the guild, or the corporative. While the

2. See Sidney and Beatrice Webb, A *Constitution for the Socialist Commonwealth of Great Britain* (London, 1920).
3. This the Webbs call "the right of self-determination for each vocation," p. 277ff.

entrepreneur of the capitalist economy is boss in his own business he nevertheless remains subject to the law of the market; if he wants to avoid losses and to make profits he has to endeavor to fulfill the wishes of the consumers as well as possible. The corporatively organized industry which would not have to fear competition would not be the servant but the master of the consumers if it were free to regulate at will the internal problems which supposedly concern it exclusively.

The majority of the proponents of the corporative state do not want to eliminate the entrepreneurs and the owners of the means of production. They want to establish the corporative as the organization of all individuals engaged in a particular line of production. Disputes between the entrepreneur, the owners of the capital invested in the industry, and the workers concerning the disposition made of gross profits and the distribution of incomes among these different groups are in their opinion merely internal problems which are to be settled autonomously within the industry without the interference of outsiders. How this is to be done, however, is never explained. If entrepreneurs, capitalists, and workers within a corporative are to be organized into separate groups or blocs, and if negotiations are to be carried on between these blocs, agreement will never be reached unless the entrepreneurs and capitalists are willing voluntarily to relinquish their rights. If, however, decisions are to be made directly or indirectly (by the election of committees) by the vote of all members with each individual having the same voting power, then the workers, being more numerous, will outvote the entrepreneurs and the capitalists and will overrule their claims. Corporativism would thus take the form of syndicalism.*

The same is true of the problem of wage scales. If this thorny question, too, is to be decided by general vote with every individual engaged in the industry having equal voting power, the result will most likely be equality of wages irrespective of the kind of work performed.

In order to have something to distribute and to pay out, the corporative must first have receipts through the sale of its products. The corpo-

---

* [Syndicalism—a movement of workers who sought to transfer to themselves the shares of entrepreneurs, owners, and capitalists in their particular industry, so that they, the workers, would own and operate the business. Their rallying cries, "The railroads to the railroadmen," "The mines to the miners" revealed their goals. For clarification, see Mises's *Human Action* (2nd–4th and Liberty Fund editions, pp. 814–816); also alphabetical entry in Percy L. Greaves, Jr.'s glossary in the Liberty Fund edition.—Editor]

rative occupies in the market the position of sole producer and seller of the goods which belong to its line. It need not be afraid of the competition of producers of identical goods because it has the exclusive right to engage in such production. We would therefore have a society of monopolists. This need not mean that all corporatives would be in a position to exact monopoly prices; but many industries would be able to exact monopoly prices and to realize monopoly profits of various amounts. The corporative organization of society will therefore give particular advantages to certain branches of production and those engaged in them. There will be industries which by restricting production will be able to increase so considerably their total receipts that those engaged in this industry will have a relatively larger share in the total consumption of the country. Some industries may even be able to achieve an absolute increase in consumption for their members despite a fall in total production.

This is sufficient to establish the shortcomings of the system of corporativism. The individual corporatives do not have any motive to make their production as efficient as possible. They are interested in reducing the output so that they may realize monopoly prices; it depends on the state of demand in the particular industry whether those engaged in the one or in the other corporative will fare better. The position of the corporatives will be the stronger the more urgent the demand for their products; the urgency of the demand will make it possible for some of them to restrict production and still to increase their total profit. The entire system would eventually lead to an unrestricted despotism of the industries producing goods which are vital in the strict sense of the word.

It is hardly to be believed that a serious attempt would ever be made to put such a system into actual operation. All proposals for a corporative system provide state intervention, at least in the case that an agreement cannot be reached between the corporatives in matters concerning several or all of them.[4] Among these matters prices certainly have to be included. It cannot be assumed that an agreement on prices could be reached between the corporatives. If the state has to intervene, however, if the state has to fix prices, then the whole system loses its corporative character and becomes either socialism or interventionism.

4. Cf. Mussolini's speech in the Italian Senate on January 13, 1934.

But the price policy is not the only point which shows that the corporative system cannot be made to work. The system renders all changes in the productive process impossible. If demand has changed or if new production methods are to replace the old ones, capital and labor have to be shifted from one industry to another. These are questions which exceed the limits of a single corporative. Here an authority superior to the corporatives has to intervene and this authority can only be the state. If, however, the state is to decide how much capital and how many workers each individual corporative is to employ, then the state is supreme, not the corporatives.

2. Syndicalism

The corporative or guild socialist system thus turns out to be syndicalism. The workers engaged in each industry are to receive control of the means of production and are to carry on production on their own account. It is unimportant whether the former entrepreneurs and capitalists are to be given a special position in the new order or not. They can no longer be entrepreneurs and capitalists in the sense in which there are entrepreneurs and capitalists in the market economy. They can only be citizens who enjoy privileges in decisions concerning management and the distribution of income. The social function, however, which they fulfilled in the market economy is taken over by the totality of the corporative. Even if in the corporative only the former entrepreneurs and capitalists had the right to make decisions and if they were to receive the largest share of the income, the system still would be syndicalism. It is not the economic characteristic of syndicalism that every syndicalist receives an equal income, or that he is consulted in questions of business policy; essential is the fact that the individuals and the means of production are rigidly attached to specific lines of production so that no worker and no factor of production is free to move from one line into another. Whether the slogan "the mills for the millers, the printing plants for the printers" is to be interpreted so that the words "millers" and "printers" are also to include the former owners of the mills and printing plants or not, and whether these former entrepreneurs and owners are given a more or less privileged position, does not matter. Decisive is that the market economy, in which the owners of the means of production and the entrepreneurs as well as the workers depend on the demands of the consumers, is being replaced by a system in which the demands of the consumers no longer determine production, but by a system in which only the wishes of the producers prevail. The cook decides what and how much each individual is to eat. Because the cook has the exclusive right to prepare food, if anyone refuses the food he is given, he would starve. Such a system might still have some meaning as long as conditions remain unchanged and as long as the distribution of capital and labor among the different lines of production corresponded to some extent to the conditions of demand. But changes are always taking place. And every change in the conditions renders the system less workable.

The postulate of syndicalism that the ownership of the means of production should be taken over by the workers is but symptomatic of the opinion of the productive process which the workers gain from the narrow perspective of their position. They regard as a permanent institution the shop in which they daily perform the same duties; they fail to realize that economic activity is subject to constant change. They do not know whether the enterprises they are working for are making profits or not. How else could the fact be explained that the employees of railroads operated at a loss demand "the railroads for the railroad employees"? The workers naively believe that only their work produces returns and that the entrepreneurs and capitalists are merely parasites. Psychologically this may explain how the ideas of syndicalism were conceived. But this understanding of the origin of the idea of syndicalism still does not turn the syndicalist program into a workable system.

The syndicalist and the corporative systems are based on the assumption that the state of production which is in effect at a given time will remain unchanged. Only if this assumption were correct would it be possible to do without shifting capital and labor from one industry into another. And to make such changes, decisions must be made by an authority superior to the single corporative and syndicate. No reputable economist therefore has ever attempted to call the syndicalist idea a satisfactory solution of the problem of social cooperation. The revolutionary syndicalism of Sorel* and of the advocates of the *action directe* have nothing to do with the syndicalist social program. Sorel's syndicalism was a system of political tactics having as its aim the attainment of socialism.

* [Georges Sorel (1847–1922), French political thinker.—Editor]

English guild socialism flourished for a brief period and then disappeared almost completely. Its original proponents themselves abandoned it, obviously because they became aware of its inherent contradictions. The corporative idea today still plays a role of some importance in the writings and in the speeches of politicians, but no nation has attempted to put it into operation. Fascist Italy, which most emphatically extols corporativism, imposes orders of the government upon all economic activity. There is therefore no room left for the existence of autonomous corporatives in "corporative" Italy.

There is a general tendency today to attribute the term "corporative" to certain institutions. Organizations which serve in an advisory capacity to the government, or cartels which are created by the governments and operate under their supervision, are called corporative institutions. But they too have nothing in common with corporativism.

However we look at it, the fact remains that the corporative or syndicalist idea cannot escape the alternative: market economy or socialism—which?

VI

War Economy

1. War and the Market Economy

Democracy is the corollary of the market economy in domestic affairs; peace is its corollary in foreign policy. The market economy means peaceful cooperation and peaceful exchange of goods and services. It cannot persist when wholesale killing is the order of the day.

The incompatibility of war with the market economy and civilization has not been fully recognized because the progressing development of the market economy has altered the original character of war itself. It has gradually turned the total war of ancient times into the soldiers' war of modern times.

Total war is a horde on the move to fight and to loot. The whole tribe, the whole people moves; no one—not even a woman or a child—remains at home unless he has to fulfill duties there essential for the war. The mobilization is total and the people are always ready to go to war. Everyone is a warrior or serves the warriors. Army and nation, army and state, are identical. No difference is made between combatants and noncombatants. The war aim is to annihilate the entire enemy nation. Total war is not terminated by a peace treaty but by a total victory and a total defeat. The defeated—men, women, children—are exterminated; it means clemency if they are merely reduced to slavery. Only the victorious nation survives.

In the soldiers' war, on the other hand, the army does the fighting while the citizens who are not in the armed services pursue their normal lives. The citizens pay the costs of warfare; they pay for the maintenance and equipment of the army, but otherwise they remain outside of the war events themselves. It may happen that the war actions raze their houses, devastate their land, and destroy their other property; but this, too, is part of the war costs which they have to bear. It may also happen that they are looted and incidentally killed by the warriors—even by those of their "own" army. But these are events which are not inherent in warfare as such; they hinder rather than help the operations of the army leaders and are not tolerated if those in command have full control over their troops. The warring state which has formed, equipped, and maintained the army considers looting by the soldiers an offense; they were hired to fight, not to loot on their own. The state wants to keep civil life as usual because it wants to preserve the taxpaying ability of its citizens; conquered territories are regarded as its own domain. The system of the market economy is to be maintained during the war to serve the requirements of warfare.

The evolution which led from the total war to the soldiers' war should have completely eliminated wars. It was an evolution whose final aim could only be eternal peace between the civilized nations. The liberals of the nineteenth century were fully aware of this fact. They considered war a remnant of a dark age which was doomed, just as were institutions of days gone by—slavery, tyranny, intolerance, superstition. They firmly believed that the future would be blessed by eternal peace.

Things have taken a different course. The development which was to bring the pacification of the world has gone into reverse. This complete reversal cannot be understood as an isolated fact. We witness today the rise of an ideology which consciously negates everything that has come to be considered as culture. The "bourgeois" values are to be revalued. The institutions of the "bourgeoisie" are to be replaced by those of the proletariat. And, in like vein, the "bourgeois" ideal of eternal peace is to be displaced by the glorification of force. The French political thinker Georges Sorel, apostle of trade unions and violence, was the godfather of both Bolshevism and Fascism.

It makes little difference that the nationalists want war between nations and that the Marxists want war between classes, i.e., civil war. What is decisive is the fact that both preach the war of annihilation, total war. It is also important if the various anti-democratic groups work in cooperation, as at present, or if they happen to be fighting each other. In either event, they are virtually always allied when it comes to attacking Western civilization.

2. Total War and War Socialism

Were we to consider as states the hordes of barbarians who descended upon the Roman Empire from the east, we would have to say that they formed total states. The horde was dominated by the political principle which the Nazis now call the Führer principle. Only the will of Attila or Alaric counted. The individual Huns or Goths had no rights and no sphere of private existence. All men, women, and children were simply units in their ruler's army or in its supply service; they had to obey unconditionally.

It would be an error to assume that these hordes were socialistically organized. Socialism is a system of social production which is based on public ownership of the means of production. These hordes did not have socialist production. Insofar as they did not live on looting the conquered but had to provide for their needs by their own work, the individual families produced with their own resources and on their own account. The ruler did not concern himself with such matters; the individual men and women were on their own. There was no planning and no socialism. The distribution of loot is not socialism.

Market economy and total war are incompatible. In the soldiers' war only the soldiers fight; for the great majority war is only a passing suffering of evil, not an active pursuit. While the armies are combating each other, the citizens, farmers, and workers try to carry on their normal activities.

The first step which led from the soldiers' war back to total war was the introduction of compulsory military service. It gradually did away with the difference between soldiers and citizens. The war was no longer to be only a matter of mercenaries; it was to include everyone who had the necessary physical ability. The slogan "a nation in arms" at first expressed only a program which could not be realized completely for financial reasons. Only part of the able-bodied male population received military training and were placed in the army services. But once this road is entered upon it is not possible to stop at halfway measures. Eventually the mobilization of the army was bound to absorb even the men indispensable to production at home who had the responsibility of feeding and equipping the combatants. It was found necessary to differentiate between essential and nonessential occupations. The men in occupations essential for supplying the army had to be exempted from induction into the combat troops. For this reason disposition of the available manpower was placed in the hands of the military leaders. Compulsory military service proposes putting everyone in the army who is able-bodied; only the ailing, the physically unfit, the old, the women, and the children are exempted. But when it is realized that a part of the able-bodied must be used on the industrial front for work which may be performed by the old and the young, the less fit and the women, then there is no reason to differentiate in compulsory service between the able-bodied and the physically unfit. Compulsory military service thus leads to compulsory labor service of all citizens who are able to work, male and female. The supreme commander exercises power over the entire nation, he replaces the work of the able-bodied by the work of less fit draftees, and places as many able-bodied at the front as he can spare at home without endangering the supplies of the army. The supreme commander then decides what is to be produced and how. He also decides how the products are to be used. Mobilization has become total; the nation and the state have been transformed into an army; war socialism has replaced the market economy.

It is irrelevant in this connection whether or not the former entrepreneurs are given a privileged position in this system of war socialism. They may be called managers and have higher positions in the factories, all of which now serve the army. They may receive larger rations than those who formerly were only clerks or laborers. But they are no longer entrepreneurs. They are shop managers who are being told what and how to produce, where and at what prices to purchase the means of production, and to whom and at what prices to sell the products.

If peace is regarded as a mere truce during which the nation has to arm itself for the coming war, it is necessary in peacetime to put production on a war footing just as much as to prepare and organize the army. It would be illogical then to delay the total mobilization until the outbreak of hostilities. The only difference between war and peace in this respect is that in time of peace a number of men, who during the war will be used in the front line, are still employed on the home front. The transition from peace conditions to war conditions is then merely the moving of those men from the home front into the army.

It is apparent that in the final analysis war and the market economy are incompatible. The market economy could only develop because industrialism had pushed militarism into the background and because it made the total war "degenerate" into the soldiers' war.

We do not need to discuss the question whether socialism necessarily leads to total war. For the subject matter with which we are here concerned such an analysis is not required. It may suffice to state that the aggressors cannot wage total war without introducing socialism.

3. Market Economy and National Defense

Today the world is divided into two camps. The totalitarian hordes are attacking the nations which seek to maintain the market economy and democracy; they are bent on destroying the "decadent" Western civilization, and to replace it by a new order.

It is believed that this aggression forces the attacked to adjust their social system to the requirements of this total war, that is to give up the market economy for socialism, and democracy for dictatorship. Despairingly one group says: "War inevitably leads to socialism and dictatorship. While we are attempting to defend democracy and to repel the attack of the enemy, we ourselves are accepting his economic order and political system." In the United States this argument is the main support for isolation. The isolationists believe that freedom can only be preserved by nonparticipation in the war.*

Exultingly the "progressives" express the same opinion. They welcome the struggle against Hitler because they are convinced that the war must bring socialism. They want American participation in the war to defeat Hitler and to introduce his system in the United States.

Is this necessarily true? Must a nation defending itself against the aggression of totalitarian countries itself become totalitarian? Is a state, which enjoyed democracy and the social system of a market economy, unable to fight a totalitarian and socialist enemy successfully?

It is widely believed that the experience of the present war proves that the socialist production is in a better position to supply arms and other war material than is a market economy. The German army has an enormous superiority in every type of equipment that a fighting army requires. The armies of France and of the British Empire, which had at their disposal the resources of the whole world, entered the conflict poorly armed and equipped and they have been unable to overcome this inferiority. These facts are undeniable, but we have to interpret them correctly.

Even at the time when the Nazis came to power the German Reich was by far better prepared for a new war than the English and French experts assumed. Since 1933 the Reich has concentrated all its efforts on preparation for war. Hitler has transformed the Reich into an armed

---

* [Remember Mises was writing in 1940, before the Japanese attacked Pearl Harbor on December 7, 1941.—Editor]

camp. War production was expanded to the limit. The production of goods for private consumption was cut to the minimum. Hitler openly prepared for a war of annihilation against France and England. The English and the French stood by as if it did not concern them at all.

During those critical years which preceded the outbreak of the second World War, there were in Europe outside of the totalitarian countries only two parties: the anti-communists and the anti-fascists. These are not names which were given to them by others or by their opponents; the parties themselves adopted these designations.

The anti-fascists—in England primarily the Labour Party, in France mainly the *front populaire*—used strong language against the Nazis. But they opposed every improvement in the armament of their own countries; in every proposal to expand the armed forces they suspected fascism. They were relying on the Soviet army, of whose strength, superior equipment, and invincibility they were convinced. What seemed to them necessary was an alliance with the Soviets. In order to win Stalin's favor, they argued, it was necessary to pursue an internal policy leaning towards Communism.

The anti-communists—the English Conservatives and the French "Right"—saw in Hitler the Siegfried who would destroy the dragon Communism. Consequently, they took a sympathetic view of Nazism. They branded as a "Jewish" lie the assertion that Hitler was planning war to annihilate France and the British Empire and aspiring to a complete domination of Europe.

The result of this policy was that England and France tumbled into the war unprepared. But still it was not too late to make good these omissions. The eight months that elapsed between the outbreak of the war and the German offensive of May 1940 would have sufficed to secure the equipment for the Allied forces which would have enabled them successfully to defend the French eastern frontier. They could have and should have utilized the powers of their industries. That they failed to do so cannot be blamed on capitalism.

One of the most popular anti-capitalist legends wants us to believe that the machinations of the munitions industry have brought about the resurgence of the war spirit. Modern imperialism and total war supposedly are the results of the war propaganda carried on by writers hired by the munitions makers. The first World War is thought to have started because Krupp, Schneider-Creuzot, DuPont, and J. P. Morgan wanted big profits. In order to avoid the recurrence of such a catastrophe, it is believed necessary to prevent the munitions industry from making profits.

On the basis of such reasoning the Blum* government nationalized the French armament industry. When the war broke out and it became imperative to place the productive power of all French plants into the service of the rearmament effort, the French authorities considered it more important to block war profits than to win the war. From September 1939 until June 1940, France in actuality did not fight the war against the Nazis, but in fact it fought a war against war profiteering. In this one respect, they were successful.

In England, too, the government was concerned primarily with preventing war profiteering, rather than with the procurement of the best possible equipment for the armed forces. For example, the 100 percent war profits tax might be cited. Even more disastrous for the Allies was the fact that in the United States, too, steps were taken to block war profits and still stronger measures of this sort were announced. This was the reason why American industry had contributed but a small part of what assistance it might have given to England and France.

The anti-capitalist says, "This is precisely the point. Business is unpatriotic. The rest of us are told to leave our families and to give up our jobs; we are placed in the army and have to risk our lives. The capitalists, however, demand their profits even in time of war. They ought to be forced to work unselfishly for the country, if we are forced to fight for it." Such arguments shift the problem into the sphere of ethics. This, however, is not a matter of ethics but of expediency.

Those who detest war on moral grounds because they consider the killing and maiming of people as inhumane should attempt to replace the ideology which leads to war by an ideology which would secure permanent peace. However, if a peaceful nation is attacked and has to defend itself, only one thing counts: The defense must be organized as quickly and as efficiently as possible; the soldiers must be given the best weapons and equipment. This can only be accomplished if the working of the market economy is not interfered with. The munitions industry, which made large profits, equipped and provisioned the armies so well in the past that they were able to win. It was due to the experiences in actual combat in the nineteenth century that the production

---

* [Léon Blum (1872–1950), French Socialist statesman who in 1936 brought about a coalition of Radical Socialists, Socialists, and Communists in the Popular Front (*front populaire*).—Editor]

of armament directly by the governments was largely discontinued. At no other time has the efficiency and productive capacity of the entrepreneurs been proved more effectively than during the first World War. It is only envy and unthinking resentment that cause people to fight against the profits of the entrepreneurs, whose efficiency makes possible the winning of the war.

When the capitalist nations in time of war give up the industrial superiority which their economic system provides them, their power to resist and their chances to win are considerably reduced. That some incidental consequences of warfare are regarded as unjust can readily be understood. The fact that entrepreneurs get rich on armament production is but one of many unsatisfactory and unjust conditions which war creates. But the soldiers risk their lives and health. That they die unknown and without reward in the front line, while the army leaders and staff remain safe and secure to win glory and to further their careers, is "unjust" too. The demand to eliminate war profits is not any more reasonable than the demand that the army leaders, their staff, the surgeons, and the men on the home front should do their work under the privations and dangers to which the fighting soldier is exposed. It is not the war profits of the entrepreneurs that are objectionable. War itself is objectionable!

These views on war profits also disclose many errors about the nature of the market economy. All those enterprises, which in peacetime already had all the necessary equipment to produce armaments and other war supplies, work from the first day of the war on government orders. But even working at full capacity, these plants can only produce a small part of the war needs. It is a question, therefore, of devoting plants to war production which previously did not produce armaments, and of actually building new factories. Both require considerable new investments. Whether or not these investments will pay depends not only on the prices realized on the first contracts but also on those contracts fulfilled during the war. Should the war end before these investments can be fully written off out of gross earnings, the owners will not only fail to realize profits, but they will even suffer capital losses. The popular argument in favor of a profitless armaments industry overlooks among other things the fact that the enterprises, which have to embark on production in a field hitherto underdeveloped by them, must obtain the capital needed from banks or in the capital market. They cannot secure it if its intended use raises no expectation of profits but only the risk of losses. How can a conscientious entrepreneur persuade a banker or a capitalist to lend him money if he himself cannot see any prospect of a profitable return on his investment? In the market economy, where the debtor has the responsibility for the repayment of the loan, there is no room for transactions which do not compensate for the risk of loss by the prospect of a gain. It is only the expectation of profit which enables an entrepreneur to promise payment of interest and repayment of principal. By eliminating the hope of profit one makes impossible the functioning of the entire system of entrepreneurship.

What is demanded of industry then is this. Give up the line in which you producers have worked successfully up to now. Do not think of the loss of your regular customers and of the depreciation of your idle equipment. Invest new capital in a line with which you are not familiar. But bear in mind, we shall pay prices which will not make it possible for you to charge off the new investment in a short time. Should you nevertheless make profits, we will tax them away. Besides, we shall publicly expose you as "merchants of death."

In war, too, there is only the choice between the market economy and socialism. The third alternative, interventionism, is not even possible in war. At the outbreak of the present war it may have been possible to nationalize the whole of industry, but there is no doubt that this would have led to a complete failure. If one did not want to adopt that method, the market economy should have been accepted with all its implications. Had the market method been chosen, the Hitler onslaught would have been stopped on the eastern borders of France. The defeat of France and the destruction of English cities was the first price paid for the interventionist suppression of war profits.

As long as the war was in progress, there should have been no place for a discussion of measures against war profits. After victory was won and a world order established in which new aggression did not have to be feared, there still would have been ample time to confiscate war profits. At any rate, before the war is over and the investments are written off, it is impossible to ascertain whether an enterprise has actually realized war profits or not.

VII

The Economic, Social, and Political Consequences of Interventionism

1. The Economic Consequences

Interventionism is not an economic system, that is, it is not a method which enables people to achieve their aims. It is merely a system of procedures which disturb and eventually destroy the market economy. It hampers production and impairs satisfaction of needs. It does not make people richer; it makes people poorer.

Concededly, the interventionist measures may give certain individuals or certain groups of individuals advantages at the expense of others. Minorities may obtain privileges which enrich them at the expense of their fellow citizens. But the majority, or the whole nation, stands only to lose by interventionism.

Let us, for instance, consider the tariff. It is quite possible to grant privileges to a group of producers, let us say the owners of copper mines; the consumers will suffer while the mine operators will gain. But if every line of production and every kind of labor is to be afforded equal protection, everyone has to give up as consumer what he gains as producer. More than that, everyone suffers because the protection shifts production from the most advantageous natural conditions, and thus diminishes the productivity of capital and labor, that is, it increases production costs. A tariff establishing just one or a few protective duties may serve the individual interests of certain groups; a comprehensive tariff system can only decrease the satisfaction of all.

But these restrictive measures are still comparatively harmless. They reduce the productivity and make people poorer but they permit the process to continue to function. The market can adjust to isolated restrictive measures. The effects are different in the case of measures designed to fix prices, wages, and interest rates at points different from what they would be in the unhampered market. If they are measures which intend the elimination of profits, they paralyze the working of the market economy. Not only do they divert production from the ways which lead to the best and most efficient satisfaction of the consumers' demand; they cause waste of both capital and labor; they create permanent mass unemployment. They may bring about the artificial boom, but with it they bring in its wake a depression. They change the market economy into chaos.

Popular opinion ascribes all these evils to the capitalistic system. As a remedy for the undesirable effects of interventionism they ask for still more interventionism. They blame capitalism for the effects of the actions of governments which pursue an anti-capitalistic policy.

The case of monopoly is particularly significant. It is possible, even probable, that in a market economy, which is unhampered by government intervention, there will be conditions which temporarily may give rise to the appearance of monopoly prices. We may regard it as probable, for instance, that even in the free-market economy an international mercury monopoly might have been formed, or that there might be local monopolies for certain building materials and fuels. But such isolated instances of monopoly prices would not yet create a "monopoly problem." All national monopolies and—with a few exceptions—all international monopolies owe their existence to tariff legislation. Were the governments really serious about fighting monopolies they would use the effective means they have at their disposal; they would remove the import duties. If they merely did this the "monopoly problem" would lose its importance. Actually, the governments are not interested in eliminating monopolies; rather, they try to create conditions to enable producers to force monopoly prices on the market.

Let us assume, for example, that the domestic plants working at full capacity produce the quantity m of a given good and that domestic consumption at the world market price p plus the import duty d (that is at the price p plus d) amounts to quantity n—n being larger than quantity m. Under such conditions the tariff will enable the domestic producers to obtain for their products a price above the world market price.[1] The protective tariff is effective; it accomplishes its purpose. This is, for instance, the case of the wheat producers in the European industrial countries. If, however, m (i.e., quantity produced) is larger

---

1. For simplicity's sake we disregard transportation costs. However, there would be no particular difficulty involved in introducing them into the calculation as well.

than the domestic consumption at world market prices, then the import duty does not give any advantage to the domestic producers. Thus, an import duty on wheat or on steel in the United States would fail to have any effect on prices; it would not by itself lead to a price increase for the domestic output of wheat or steel.

If, however, the domestic producers want to obtain advantages from the tariff protection even when m is larger than the domestic consumption at world market prices, they have to form a cartel, a trust, or some other form of monopolistic combination and agree to reduce production. Then they are in a position, provided the state of demand (the shape of the demand curve) permits it, to force the consumer to pay monopoly prices which are higher than world market prices, but lower than the world market price plus the import duty. What in the first instance is attained directly by the tariff must in the second case be accomplished by the monopoly organization which the protective tariff makes possible.

Most of the international cartels were only made possible because the totality of the world market was separated into national economic areas by tariffs and related measures. How insincere the governments are in their attitude toward monopolies is most evident in their efforts to create world monopolies, even for articles for which the conditions required to form monopolies call for special measures over and above tariff legislation. The economic history of the last decade shows a number of measures of different governments designed—though not successfully—to create world monopolies for sugar, rubber, coffee, tin, and other commodities.

To the extent that interventionism accomplishes the aims which government is seeking, it also creates an artificial scarcity of goods and price increases. As far as the governments pursue other than these two aims, they fail; rather, effects appear which the governments themselves consider even less desirable than the conditions they tried to remove. Out of this chaos to which interventionism leads, there are only two ways of escape—the return to an unhampered market or the adoption of socialism.

The unhampered market economy is not a system which would seem commendable from the standpoint of the selfish group interests of the entrepreneurs and capitalists. It is not the particular interests of a group or of individual persons that require the market economy, but regard for the common welfare. It is not true that the advocates of the free-market economy are defenders of the selfish interests of the rich. The particular interests of the entrepreneurs and capitalists also demand interventionism to protect them against the competition of more efficient and active men. The free development of the market economy is to be recommended, not in the interest of the rich, but in the interest of the masses of the people.

2. Parliamentary Government and Interventionism

Government by the people is based on the idea that all citizens are linked by common interests. The framers of the modern constitutions did not overlook the fact that in the short run the particular interests of individual groups may conflict with those of the overwhelming majority. But they had full confidence in the intelligence of their fellow citizens. They did not doubt that their fellow citizens would be wise enough to realize that selfish group interests must be sacrificed when they run counter to the welfare of the majority. They were convinced that every group would recognize that privileges cannot be maintained in the long run. Privileges are only of value if they benefit a minority; they lose value as they become more general. When every individual group of citizens is granted privileges, the privileges as such become meaningless; everybody suffers, nobody gains.

Government by the people can, therefore, only be maintained under the system of the market economy. In the market economy only the interests of the citizens as consumers are considered. No producer is granted a privilege, because privileges given to producers diminish productivity and impair the satisfaction of the consumers. No one suffers if the cheapest and best satisfaction of the consumers is accepted as the guiding principle of policy; what producers then fail to gain as producers, because privileges are denied to them, they gain as consumers.

Every technological progress first injures vested interests of entrepreneurs, capitalists, landowners, or workers. But if the desire to prevent such injuries is to prompt measures to prevent the development of new techniques, this would in the long run harm not only the interests of all citizens, but also of those who supposedly were to be benefited. The automobile and the airplane hurt the railway business, the radio hurts the publishing business, the motion pictures the legitimate theater.

Should automobiles, planes, broadcasting, and movies have been forbidden in order to spare the interests of the injured entrepreneurs, capitalists, and workers? It was the great achievement of the old liberalism that it abolished the privileges of the guilds and thus opened the way for modern industry. If there are today many more people on earth than two hundred years ago and if every worker in the countries of Western civilization lives today far better than his ancestors, in some respects even better than Louis XIV in his palace at Versailles, then this is only due to this liberation of the productive forces.

The idea underlying representative government is that the members of parliament are to represent the whole nation, not to represent individual counties or the particular interests of their constituencies. The political parties may represent different opinions about what helps the whole nation, but they should not represent the particular selfish interests of certain districts or pressure groups.

The parliaments of interventionist countries are today quite different from this old ideal. There are representatives of silver, cotton, steel, farming, and labor. But no legislator feels it his duty to represent the nation as a whole.

The democratic form of government which Hitler destroyed in Germany and France was not workable because it was thoroughly infested with the interventionist spirit. There were many small parties which catered to particular local and professional interests. Every proposed bill and every executive measure was judged by one standard: What does it offer my constituents and the pressure groups on which I depend? The representatives of a wine-producing district considered everything from the standpoint of the wine producers. Questions of national defense were for the labor representatives nothing but an opportunity to enhance the power of the trade unions. The spokesmen of the French *front populaire* demanded cooperation with Russia, those of the Right an alliance with Italy. Neither group was concerned with the welfare and the independence of France; in every problem they saw only its relation to, and effect on, the particular interests of particular voting blocks. Interventionism has transformed parliamentary government into a government of lobbies. It is not parliamentarianism and democracy that have failed. Interventionism has paralyzed parliamentarianism as well as the market economy.

The failure of parliamentarianism becomes more evident in the practice of delegating authority. The parliament voluntarily gives up its legislative power and hands it over to the executive. Hitler, Mussolini, and Pétain* govern by such "delegations of power." The dictatorship thus assumed a vestige of legality by a formal link to the democratic institutions. It abolished democracy and retained the democratic terminology, just as in the system of German socialism it abolished private property while retaining its nomenclature. The tyrants of the cities of ancient Greece and the Roman Caesars, too, preserved the phraseology of the Republic.

At the present stage in the development of the means of communication and transportation no emergency can justify the delegation of power. Even in a large country like the United States, all representatives can be assembled in the capital within 24 hours. It would also be possible to have the representative bodies remain in permanent session. Whenever it appeared advisable to keep secret the proceedings and decisions, secret sessions could be held.

Frequently, we hear the assertion that the democratic institutions are only a disguise for the "dictatorship of capital." The Marxists have used this slogan for a long time. Georges Sorel and the syndicalists repeated it. Today Hitler and Mussolini ask the nations to rise up against "plutodemocracy." In answer to this it suffices to point out that in Great Britain, in the British Dominions, and in the United States the elections are completely free of coercion. Franklin D. Roosevelt was elected president by a majority of the voters. Nobody forced any American citizen to vote for him. Nobody prevented anyone from voicing publicly what he considered an argument against the reelection of Roosevelt. The citizens of America were free to decide, and they did decide.

3. Freedom and the Economic System

The first argument advanced against proposals to replace capitalism by socialism was that in the socialist economic system there could be no room for freedom of the individual. Socialism, it was said, means slavery for all. It is impossible to deny the truth of this argument. If the government controls all means of production, if the government is the only employer and has the sole right to decide what training the

---

* [Henri Philippe Pétain (1856–1951), French World War I hero, vice premier in June 1940 when Germany defeated and occupied half of France, became "chief of state" of the fascist unoccupied portion of the country, with its capital at Vichy. After the war he was tried and convicted of collaborating with the Germans.—Editor]

individual is to receive, where and how he is to work, then the individual is not free. He has the duty to obey, but he has no rights.

The advocates of socialism have never been able to present an effective counterargument to this. They have merely retorted that in the democratic countries of the market economy there was only freedom for the rich, not for the poor, and that for such freedom it was not worth renouncing the supposed blessings of socialism.

In order to analyze these questions we first have to understand what freedom really means. Freedom is a sociological concept. In nature and with regard to nature there is nothing to which we could apply this term. Freedom is the opportunity granted to the individual by the social system to mold his life according to his wishes. That people have to work in order to survive is a law of nature; no social system can alter this fact. That the rich may live without working does not impair the freedom of those who are not in this fortunate position. Wealth in the market economy represents rewards granted by society as a whole for services rendered to the consumers in the past, and it can only be preserved by continued employment in the interest of the consumers. That the market economy rewards successful activity in the service of the consumers does not harm the consumers; it benefits them. Nothing is taken from the worker by this, but much is given to him by increasing the productivity of labor. The freedom of the worker who does not own property rests on his right to choose the place and the type of his work. He does not have an overlord to whose arbitrariness he is subjected. He sells his services on the market. If one entrepreneur refuses to pay him the wage which corresponds to the market conditions he will find another employer who is willing, out of his (the employer's) own interest, to pay the worker the market wage. The worker does not owe his employer subservience and obedience; he owes him services; he receives his wage not as a favor, but as an earned reward.

The poor too have an opportunity in the capitalistic society to work themselves up through their own efforts. This is not the case only in business. Among those who today occupy top positions in the professions, in art, science, and politics, the majority are men who have started their careers in poverty. Among the path-breakers and leaders there are men born almost exclusively from poor parents. Those who want great accomplishments, no matter what the social system, must overcome the resistance of apathy, prejudice, and ignorance. It can hardly be denied that capitalism offers this opportunity.

Instances are pointed out where great men were badly treated by their contemporaries. Some of the great masters of the French modern school of painting have experienced great difficulties or were not able to sell their paintings at all. Does anyone believe that a socialist government would show more understanding for an art which appeared to traditional concepts as so much scribbling? The great composer Hugo Wolf* once wrote it was a shame that the state did not provide for its artists. But what Hugo Wolf suffered from was a lack of understanding on the part of the recognized older artists, critics, and friends of art; a socialist government would have had to rely on the judgment of state-appointed experts and it certainly would not have given more recognition to that irritable, unsociable, and mentally unbalanced man. When Sigmund Freud† advanced his theories, the established authorities, doctors, and psychologists, that is the experts whose judgment must be decisive for the government, laughed and called him crazy.

But in the capitalistic society the genius at least has an opportunity to continue his work.

The great French painters were free to paint; Hugo Wolf was in a position to put Moerike's‡ poems to music; Freud was free to continue his studies. They would not have been able to produce anything if the government, following the unanimous opinion of the experts, had assigned them work which deprived them of the opportunity to fulfill their destiny.

Unfortunately, it happens not infrequently that, for political reasons, the universities fail to appoint as professors outstanding men in the fields of social science, or they dismiss them after they have been appointed. But are we to believe that the state university of a socialist country would employ men who taught doctrines unpleasing to the government? In the socialist state publishing, too, is a function of the state. Will the state have books and papers printed and published with which it disagrees? Will it make available to the stage dramas which it thinks inappropriate?

Compare the position in which science, art, literature, the press, and radio find themselves in Russia and Germany with their positions in America; then we will understand what freedom and lack of freedom

---

* [Hugo Wolf (1860–1903), Viennese composer and music critic, spent the last seven years of his life in a mental asylum.—Editor]
† [Sigmund Freud (1856–1939), Viennese founder of psychoanalysis.—Editor]
‡ [Eduard Moerike (1804–1875), German Protestant minister and poet.—Editor]

mean. Many things appear unsatisfactory in America as well, but no one will be able to deny that the Americans are freer than the Russians or the Germans.

The freedom of scientific and artistic creation is actively made use of by only a small minority, but all benefit from it. Progress is always displacement of the old by the new; progress always means change. No planned economy can plan progress; no organization can organize it. It is the one thing that defies any limitation or regimentation. State and society cannot promote progress. Capitalism cannot do anything for progress either. But, and this is achievement enough, capitalism doesn't place insurmountable barriers in the way of progress. The socialist society would become utterly rigid because it would make progress impossible.

Interventionism does not take all freedom from the citizens. But every one of its measures takes away a part of the freedom and narrows the field of activity.

Let us consider, for instance, foreign exchange control. The smaller a country, the more important the part played in its total trade by foreign transactions. If subscriptions to foreign books and newspapers, foreign travel and study abroad, are made conditional upon the granting of foreign exchange by the government, the entire intellectual life of the country comes under the guardianship of the government. In this respect foreign exchange control is not at all different from the despotic system of Prince Metternich.* The only difference is that Metternich did openly what foreign exchange control effects through disguise.

4. The Great Delusion

It cannot be denied that dictatorship, interventionism, and socialism are extremely popular today. No argument of logic can weaken this popularity. The fanatics obstinately refuse to listen to the teachings of economic theory. Experience fails to teach them anything. They stubbornly adhere to their previous opinions.

To understand the roots of this stubbornness we have to keep in mind that people suffer because things do not always happen the way they want them to. Man is born as an asocial selfish being and only

---

* [Prince Klemens W. N. L. von Metternich (1773–1859), Austrian statesman, relied on censorship, espionage, and repression to control much of Europe.—Editor]

in actual living does he learn that his will does not stand alone in the world and that there are other people too who have their own wills. Only life and experience teach him that in order to realize *his* plans he has to fit himself into the whole of society, that he has to accept other people's wills and wishes as facts, and that he has to adjust himself to these facts in order to achieve anything at all. Society is not what the individual would want it to be. The fellowmen of any particular individual have a lesser opinion of him than he has of himself. They do not accord him the place in society which, in his opinion, he thinks he should have. Every day brings the conceited—and who is entirely free of conceit?—new disappointments. Every day shows him that his will conflicts with those of other people.

From these disappointments the neurotic takes refuge in daydreams. He dreams of a world in which his will alone is decisive. In this world of dreams he is dictator. Only what he approves of happens. He alone gives orders; the others obey. His reason alone is supreme.

In that secret world of dreams the neurotic assumes the role of dictator. There he is Caesar, Genghis Khan, Napoleon. When in real life he speaks to his fellow men he has to be more modest. He contents himself with approving a dictatorship which someone else rules. But in his mind this dictator is merely his, that is, the neurotic's, order-taker; he assumes the dictator will do precisely what he, the neurotic, wants him to do. A man who did not apply caution and who suggested that he become the dictator himself would be considered insane by his fellow men and would be treated accordingly. The psychiatrists would call him a megalomaniac.

No one has ever favored a dictatorship to do things other than what he, the supporter of the dictatorship, considers right. Those who recommend dictatorships always have in mind the unchecked domination of their own will, even if this domination is to be implemented by someone else.

Let us examine, for instance, the slogan "planned economy," which today is a particularly popular pseudonym for socialism. Everything that people do must first be conceived, that is it must be planned. Every economy is in this sense a planned economy. But those who, with Marx, reject the "anarchy of production" and want to replace it by "planning" do not consider the will and the plans of others. One will alone is to decide; one plan alone is to be executed, namely the plan which meets with the neurotic's approval, the right plan, the *only* plan.

Any resistance is to be broken; no one is to prevent the poor neurotic from arranging the world according to his own plans; every means is to be permitted to assure that the superior wisdom of the daydreamer prevails.

This is the mentality of the people who once in the art exhibits of Paris exclaimed on viewing the paintings of Manet*: The police ought not to allow this! This is the mentality of the people who constantly cry: There should be a law against this! And whether they recognize it or not this is the mentality of all interventionists, socialists, and advocates of dictatorship. There is but one thing they hate more than capitalism, namely interventionism, socialism, or dictatorship which does not conform to their will. How ardently have Nazis and Communists fought each other! How determinedly do the partisans of Trotsky† fight those of Stalin, or the followers of Strasser‡ those of Hitler!

5. The Source of Hitler's Success

Hitler, Stalin, and Mussolini constantly proclaim that they are chosen by destiny to bring salvation to this world. They claim they are the leaders of the creative youth who fight against their outlived elders. They bring from the East the new culture which is to replace the dying Western civilization. They want to give the *coup de grâce* to liberalism and capitalism; they want to overcome immoral egoism by altruism; they plan to replace the anarchic democracy by order and organization, the society of "classes" by the total state, the market economy by socialism. Their war is not a war for territorial expansion, for loot and hegemony like the imperialistic wars of the past, but a holy crusade for a better world to live in. And they feel certain of their victory because they are convinced that they are borne by "the wave of the future."

It is a law of nature, they say, that great historic changes cannot take place peacefully or without conflict. It would be petty and stupid, they contend, to overlook the creative quality of their work because of some unpleasantness which the great world revolution must necessarily bring with it. They maintain one should not overlook the glory of

* [Edouard Manet (1832–1883), French impressionist painter.—Editor]
† [Leon Trotsky (1879–1940), Russian Communist who opposed Stalin and was forced into exile. He went to Mexico where he was murdered in August 1940.—Editor]
‡ [Gregor Strasser (1892–1934), an early supporter of Hitler who later differed with him and was murdered.—Editor]

the new gospel because of ill-placed pity for Jews and Masons, Poles and Czechs, Finns and Greeks, the decadent English aristocracy and the corrupt French bourgeoisie. Such softness and such blindness for the new standards of morality prove only the decadence of the dying capitalistic pseudo-culture. The whining and crying of impotent old men, they say, is futile; it will not stop the victorious advance of youth. No one can stop the wheel of history, or turn back the clock of time.

The success of this propaganda is overwhelming. People do not consider the content of alleged new gospel; they merely understand that it is new and believe to see in this fact its justification. As women welcome a new style in clothes just to have a change, so the supposedly new style in politics and economics is welcomed. People hasten to exchange their "old" ideas for "new" ones, because they fear to appear old-fashioned and reactionary. They join the chorus decrying the shortcomings of the capitalistic civilization and speak in elated enthusiasm of the achievements of the autocrats. Nothing is today more fashionable than slandering Western civilization.

This mentality has made it easy for Hitler to gain his victories. The Czechs and the Danes capitulated without a fight. Norwegian officers handed over large sections of their country to Hitler's army. The Dutch and the Belgians gave in after only a short resistance. The French had the audacity to celebrate the destruction of their independence as a "national revival." It took Hitler five years to effect the *Anschluss* of Austria; two-and-one-half years later he was master of the European continent.

Hitler does not have a new secret weapon at his disposal. He does not owe his victory to an excellent intelligence service which informs him of the plans of his opponents. Even the much-talked-of "fifth column" was not decisive. He won because the supposed opponents were already quite sympathetic to the ideas for which he stood.

Only those who unconditionally and unrestrictedly consider the market economy as the only workable form of social cooperation are opponents of the totalitarian systems and are capable of fighting them successfully. Those who want socialism intend to bring to their country the system which Russia and Germany enjoy. To favor interventionism means to enter a road which inevitably leads to socialism.

An ideological struggle cannot be fought successfully with constant concessions to the principles of the enemy. Those who refute capitalism because it supposedly is inimical to the interest of the masses, those who proclaim "as a matter of course" that after the victory over

Hitler the market economy will have to be replaced by a better system and, therefore, everything should be done now to make the government control of business as complete as possible, are actually fighting for totalitarianism. The "progressives" who today masquerade as "liberals" may rant against "fascism"; yet it is their policy that paves the way for Hitlerism.

Nothing could have been more helpful to the success of the National-Socialist (Nazi) movement than the methods used by the "progressives," denouncing Nazism as a party serving the interests of "capital." The German workers knew this tactic too well to be deceived by it again. Was it not true that, since the seventies of the [nineteenth] century, the ostensibly pro-labor Social-Democrats had fought all the pro-labor measures of the German government vigorously, calling them "bourgeois" and injurious to the interests of the working class? The Social-Democrats had consistently voted against the nationalization of the railroads, the municipalization of the public utilities, labor legislation, and compulsory accident, sickness, and old-age insurance, the German social security system which was adopted later throughout the world. Then after the war [World War I] the Communists branded the German Social-Democratic party and the Social-Democratic unions as "traitors to their class." So the German workers realized that every party wooing them called the competing parties "willing servants of capitalism," and their allegiance to Nazism would not be shattered by such phrases.

Unless we are utterly oblivious to the facts, we must realize that the German workers are the most reliable supporters of the Hitler regime. Nazism has won them over completely by eliminating unemployment and by reducing the entrepreneurs to the status of shop managers (*Betriebsführer*). Big business, shopkeepers, and peasants are disappointed. Labor is well satisfied and will stand by Hitler, unless the war takes a turn which would destroy their hope for a better life after the peace treaty. Only military reverses can deprive Hitler of the backing of the German workers.

The fact that the capitalists and entrepreneurs, faced with the alternative of Communism or Nazism, chose the latter, does not require any further explanation. They preferred to live as shop managers under Hitler than to be "liquidated" as "bourgeois" by Stalin. Capitalists don't like to be killed any more than other people do.

What pernicious effects may be produced by believing that the German workers are opposed to Hitler was proved by the English tactics during the first year of the war. The government of Neville Chamberlain* firmly believed that the war would be brought to an end by a revolution of the German workers. Instead of concentrating on vigorous arming and fighting, they had their planes drop leaflets over Germany telling the German workers that England was not fighting this war against *them,* but against their oppressor, Hitler. The English government knew very well, they said, that the German people, particularly labor, were against war and were only forced into it by their self-imposed dictator.

The workers in the Anglo-Saxon countries, too, knew that the socialist parties competing for their favor usually accused each other of favoring capitalism. Communists of all shades advance this accusation against socialists. And within the Communist groups the Trotskyites used this same argument against Stalin and his men. And vice versa. The fact that the "progressives" bring the same accusation against Nazism and Fascism will not prevent labor someday from following another gang wearing shirts of a different color.

What is wrong with Western civilization is the accepted habit of judging political parties merely by asking whether they seem new and radical enough, not by analyzing whether they are wise or unwise, or whether they are apt to achieve their aims. Not everything that exists today is reasonable; but this does not mean that everything that does not exist is sensible.

The usual terminology of political language is stupid. What is "left" and what is "right"? Why should Hitler be "right" and Stalin, his temporary friend, be "left"?† Who is "reactionary" and who is "progressive"? Reaction against an unwise policy is not to be condemned. And progress towards chaos is not to be commended. Nothing should find acceptance just because it is new, radical, and fashionable. "Orthodoxy" is not an evil if the doctrine on which the "orthodox" stand is sound. Who is anti-labor, those who want to lower labor to the Russian level, or those who want for labor the capitalistic standard of the United States?

* [Neville Chamberlain (1869–1940) was British prime minister from 1937 to May 1940.—Editor]

† [Remember that when Mises wrote this in 1940, Hitler and Stalin were allies under the terms of their August 1939 mutual nonaggression treaty.—Editor]

Who is "nationalist," those who want to bring their nation under the heel of the Nazis, or those who want to preserve its independence?

What would have happened to Western civilization if its peoples had always shown such liking for the "new"? Suppose they had welcomed as "the wave of the future" Attila and his Huns, the creed of Mohammed, or the Tartars? They, too, were totalitarian and had military successes to their credit which made the weak hesitate and ready to capitulate. What mankind needs today is liberation from the rule of nonsensical slogans and a return to sound reasoning.

VIII.

Conclusions

This essay does not deal with the question whether socialism—public ownership of the means of production, a planned economy—is in any way a system superior to capitalism or whether socialism represents a feasible workable system of social cooperation at all. It does not discuss the programs of those parties that want to replace capitalism, democracy, and freedom by socialist totalitarianism according to either the Russian or the German pattern. The author has dealt with these questions in another book.[1] Nor is this analysis concerned with whether democratic government and civil liberties are good or bad. Or whether or not totalitarian dictatorship is a better form of government.

This analysis is intended merely to explain that the economic policy of interventionism, which is advertised by its advocates as a progressive socioeconomic policy, is based on a fallacy. This book demonstrates that it is not true that interventionism can lead to a lasting system of economic organization. The various measures by which interventionism tries to direct business cannot achieve the aims its honest advocates are seeking by their application. Interventionist measures lead to conditions which, from the standpoint of those who recommend them, are actually less desirable than those they are designed to alleviate. They create unemployment, depression, monopoly, distress. They may make a few people richer, but they make all others poorer and less satisfied. If governments do not give them up and return to the unhampered market economy, if they stubbornly persist in the attempt to compensate by further interventions for the shortcomings of earlier interventions, they will find eventually that they have adopted socialism.

Furthermore, it is a tragic error to believe that democracy and freedom are compatible with interventionism or even with socialism.

1. *Socialism*, English translation, 1936 [Yale, 1951; Jonathan Cape, 1969; Liberty Fund, 1981].

What people mean by democratic government, civil liberties, and personal freedom can exist only in the market economy. It is not an accident that everywhere, with the progress of interventionism, the democratic institutions have disappeared one after the other and that, in the socialist countries, oriental despotism has been able to stage a successful comeback. It is not mere chance that democracy is attacked everywhere, both by the partisans of Russian Communism and by those of German Socialism. The radicalism of the "right" and the radicalism of the "left" differ in minor unimportant details only; they meet in their wholesale denunciations of both capitalism and democracy.

Mankind has a choice only between the unhampered market economy, democracy, and freedom on the one side, and socialism and dictatorship on the other side. A third alternative, an interventionist compromise, is not feasible.

It may be pointed out that this conclusion is in accord with some of the teachings of Karl Marx and orthodox Marxists. Marx and the Marxists have branded as "petit bourgeois" all those measures which are called interventionism, and they have acknowledged their self-contradictory character. Marx considered it futile for trade unions to try to obtain higher wages for the whole working class in the capitalistic society. And the orthodox Marxists have always protested against proposals to have the state, directly or indirectly, fix minimum-wage rates. Marx developed the doctrine that a "dictatorship of the proletariat" was necessary to prepare the way for socialism, the "higher phase of communist society." During the transition period of several centuries there would be no room for democracy. Thus, Lenin was quite right when he pointed to Marx to justify his reign of terror. As to what would happen after socialism was attained, Marx merely said that the state would wither away.

The victories which Lenin, Mussolini, and Hitler have won were not defeats of capitalism but the inescapable consequences of interventionist policy. Lenin defeated the interventionism of Kerensky.* Mussolini won his victory over the syndicalism of the Italian trade unions which culminated in the seizure of factories. Hitler triumphed over the interventionism of the Weimar Republic. Franco† won his victory over the

---

* [Aleksandr Kerensky (1881–1970), Russian politician, was the leader of the Russian government after the March 1917 Revolution, which deposed the czar. He fled Russia when his faction was defeated by the Bolsheviks during the October 1917 Revolution.—Editor]
† [Francisco Franco (1892–1975), Spanish general and dictator who assumed power in 1939 at the conclusion of the Spanish Civil War.—Editor]

syndicalist anarchy in Spain and Catalonia. In France the system of the *front populaire* collapsed and the dictatorship of Pétain followed. Once interventionism was embarked upon, this was the logical sequence of events. Interventionism will always lead to the same result.

If there is anything history could teach us it would be that no nation has ever created a higher civilization without private ownership of the means of production and that democracy has only been found where private ownership of the means of production has existed.

Should our civilization perish, it will not be because it is doomed, but because people refused to learn from theory or from history. It is not fate that determines the future of human society, but man himself. The decay of Western civilization is not an act of God, something which cannot be averted. If it comes, it will be the result of a policy which still can be abandoned and replaced by a better policy.

READING REFERENCES

In this book, Mises shows how government intervention results in consequences its proponents did not intend. It hampers production, causing artificial scarcities. It creates special interest groups. It leads to inflation, domestic economic conflict, a militant nationalism, international conflict, and even war. The books listed here deal with various aspects of intervention and help to elaborate and expand on Mises's theme.

Bastiat, Frederic. *Economic Sophisms* (French original, 1845, 1848; translated by Arthur Goddard, Van Nostrand, 1964). Irvington-on-Hudson, N.Y.: Foundation for Economic Education, 1991.

Carson, Clarence B. *Flight from Reality.* Irvington-on-Hudson, N.Y.: Foundation for Economic Education, 1969.

———. *The World in the Grip of an Idea.* New Rochelle, N.Y.: Arlington House, 1980.

Friedman, Milton, with the assistance of Rose D. Friedman. *Capitalism and Freedom* (1962). New preface by the author. Chicago: University of Chicago Press, 1982.

Greaves, Percy L., Jr. *Understanding the Dollar Crisis* (1973). Dobbs Ferry, N.Y.: Free Market Books, 1984.

Hayek, F. A. *The Road to Serfdom* (1944). 50th anniversary edition with a new introduction by Milton Friedman. Chicago: University of Chicago Press, 1994.

Hazlitt, Henry. *Economics in One Lesson* (1946; many reprints). 50th anniversary edition. Foreword by Steve Forbes. San Francisco: Laissez Faire Books, 1996.

Higgs, Robert. *Crisis and Leviathan: Critical Episodes in the Growth of American Government.* New York: Oxford University Press, 1987.

Mises, Ludwig von. *Bureaucracy* (1944; reprinted 1969). Spring Mills, Pa.: Libertarian Press, 1983.

———. *Economic Policy: Thoughts for Today and Tomorrow* (1979). Irvington-on-Hudson, N.Y.: Free Market Books, 1995.

———. *Liberalism: The Classical Tradition* (German original, 1927; translated by Ralph Raico; 1st English-language edition titled *The Free and Prosperous Commonwealth*, 1962). Irvington-on-Hudson, N.Y.: Foundation for Economic Education, 1985, 1996.

———. *Nation, State and Economy: Contributions to the Politics and History of Our Time* (German original, 1919; translated by Leland B. Yeager). New York: New York University Press, 1983.

———. *Omnipotent Government: The Rise of the Total State and Total War* (1944; 1969). Spring Mills, Pa.: Libertarian Press, 1985.

———. *Planned Chaos.* Irvington-on-Hudson, N.Y.: Foundation for Economic Education, 1947. Many printings. Included as the "Epilogue" in 1951 and later editions of Mises's *Socialism* (Yale, 1951; Jonathan Cape, 1969; and Liberty Fund, 1981).

Opitz, Edmund A., ed. *Leviathan at War.* Irvington-on-Hudson, N.Y.: Foundation for Economic Education, Inc., 1995.

Ortega y Gasset, José. *The Revolt of the Masses* (Spanish original, 1930; authorized English translation, 1932). New York: W. W. Norton, 1993.

Röpke, Wilhelm. *The Social Crisis of Our Time* (German original, 1942; English translation, 1950). Introduction by William F. Campbell, foreword by Russell Kirk. New Brunswick, N.J.: Transaction Books, 1992.

———. *Welfare, Freedom and Inflation.* Foreword by Roger A. Freeman, introduction by Graham Hutton. University, Ala.: University of Alabama Press, 1964.

Rothbard, Murray N. *What Has Government Done to Our Money?* (1964, 1974). Auburn, Ala.: Ludwig von Mises Institute/Auburn University, 1990.

Rummel, R. J. *Death by Government.* Foreword by Irving Louis Horowitz. New Brunswick, N.J.: Transaction Publishers, 1994.

———. *Power Kills: Democracy as a Method of Nonviolence.* New Brunswick, N.J.: Transaction Publishers, 1997.

Sennholz, Hans F. *Age of Inflation.* Belmont, Mass.: Western Islands, 1979.

———. *Money and Freedom.* Spring Mills, Pa.: Libertarian Press, 1985.

Sowell, Thomas. *Knowledge and Decisions.* New York: Basic Books, 1980.

Stolper, Gustav. *German Economy: 1870–1940. Issues and Trends.* New York: Reynal Hitchcock, 1940.

Sulzbach, Walter. *National Consciousness.* Introduction by Hans Kohn. Washington, D.C.: American Council on Public Affairs, 1943.

Taylor, Joan Kennedy, ed. *Free Trade: The Necessary Foundation of World Peace* (1986). Irvington-on-Hudson, N.Y.: Foundation for Economic Education, 1996.

INDEX

The typeface used in setting this book is Electra, designed in 1935 by the great American typographer William Addison Dwiggins. Dwiggins was a student and associate of Frederic Goudy and served for a time as acting director of Harvard University Press. In his illustrious career as typographer and book designer (he coined the term "graphic designer"), Dwiggins created a number of typefaces, including Metro and Caledonia, and designed as well many of the typographic ornaments or "dingbats" familiar to readers.

Electra is a crisp, elegant, and readable typeface, strongly suggestive of calligraphy. The contrast between its strokes is relatively muted, and it produces an even but still "active" impression in text. Interestingly, the design of the *italic* form—called "cursive" in this typeface—is less calligraphic than the italic form of many faces, and more closely resembles the roman.

This book is printed on paper that is acid-free and meets the requirements of the American National Standard for Permanence of Paper for Printed Library Materials, z39.48–1992. ∞

Book design adapted by Erin Kirk New, Watkinsville, Georgia, after a design by Martin Lubin Graphic Design, Jackson Heights, New York

Typography by G&S Typesetters, Inc., Austin, Texas

Printed and bound by Malloy Incorporated, Ann Arbor, Michigan